FLIP *the* STORY

Saloni Malhotra
&
Astha Ahluwalia

A Grin Presentation

FLIP *the* STORY

Saloni Malhotra & Astha Ahluwalia

First published in 2024 by **Grin**
an imprint of Grin Media Private Limited

Milap Niketan, 8A, Bahadur Shah Zafar Marg, New Delhi, Delhi-110002
www.globalorder.live || www.grin.news

ISBN 978-81-977979-5-8

Printed and Bound in India R. K. Print Solution.

This book is dedicated to

Mum & Dad

and

Sarita and Ashwani Anand

For sowing the seeds of Reboot and nurturing us

The Guest House

By Rumi

This being human is a guest house.
Every morning a new arrival.

A joy, a depression, a meanness,
some momentary awareness comes
As an unexpected visitor.

Welcome and entertain them all!
Even if they're a crowd of sorrows,
who violently sweep your house
empty of its furniture,
still treat each guest honorably.
He may be clearing you out
for some new delight.

The dark thought, the shame, the malice,
meet them at the door laughing,
and invite them in.

Be grateful for whoever comes,
because each has been sent
as a guide from beyond.

Advance Praise

'Flip The Story, provides a powerful toolkit to reframe your thoughts and emotions, and turn challenges into opportunities for healing and self-discovery. An essential read for anyone who's ready to take control of their inner narrative and turn it into growth.'

– Kunal Kapoor, Actor

'It's a reminder that with the right mindset, we can turn even our most challenging experiences into moments of growth.'

– Vijay Shekhar Sharma, Founder & CEO, Paytm

'If you've ever felt down or stuck in a low cycle, this book will teach you how to flip your mindset and turn obstacles into opportunities. A practical and insightful guide for those ready to take control of their emotional well-being. A must have for all those who wish to live life filled with positivity!'

– Dr Shikha Sharma, Founder & CEO, NutriHealth

'As someone who has long explored the depths of the human mind, I can say without hesitation that 'Flip The Story' is a profound and timely contribution to the conversation on mental health. Saloni and Astha deftly guide readers through the process of reframing their narratives, and reclaiming their story with clarity and strength. A must-read for anyone looking to find growth and meaning amidst life's complexities.'

– Shuchi Singh, Bestselling Author of 'I Am Big, So What?' and 'Done with Men'

'Flip The Story is a masterclass in emotional resilience. With clarity and compassion, it teaches us that while we may not always control life's circumstances, we can control how we respond. This book provides the tools to navigate our inner world and, most importantly, to emerge stronger from our struggles.'

– Kiran Pasricha, former CEO, Ananta Aspen Centre

'I believe that the ability to write and rewrite our life story, over and over again, is the ultimate super power and freedom we all have. This books shines a light on this super power in a gentle and simple language, capturing not just the challenge but also the opportunity for self-discovery and inner strength. Our emotions are what makes us human and if all of us paid more attention to our emotions.. the world would be a much better place.'

– Anshu Gupta, Founder and CEO, Goonj

Contents

Introduction

> ***Our life is what our thoughts make it. A man will find that as he alters his thoughts toward things and other people, things and other people will alter towards him.***
>
> ***– Marcus Aurelius***

You've probably heard the parable:

An old Cherokee is teaching his grandson about life. "A fight is going on inside me," he said to the boy. "It is a terrible fight and it is between two wolves. One is evil – he is anger, envy, sorrow, regret, greed, arrogance, self-pity, guilt, resentment, inferiority, lies, false pride, superiority, and ego."

He continued, "The other is good – he is joy, peace, love, hope, serenity, humility, kindness, benevolence, empathy, generosity, truth, compassion, and faith. The same fight is going on inside you – and inside every other person, too."

The grandson thought about it for a minute and then asked his grandfather, "Which wolf will win?"

The old Cherokee simply replied, "The one you feed."

From Saloni

I had recommended a dear friend of mine to the therapists at Reboot. After three months of hard work on our weekly Fabulous Friday night sessions, I asked her how therapy had helped her and she replied with a smile, "I came in as an angry person and I am walking out as a curious individual."

We both knew that this simple flip had been hard, almost inconceivable three months ago. And as we chatted more into the evening I kept going back to flipping anger with curiosity. Over the two decades of knowing each other, as all good friends, we had our own language. "Fix the Signal to Noise Ratio" was our way to let each other know that we were struggling with something – a situation, a decision or sometimes just a conversation. And then we would think, together, about what was a good filter to pass the signal that would block the noise. Curiosity was her filter this time to deal with anger.

What were the other common noisy stories in our head? What were the filters that would flip these stories? I went back home that night and made a list of emotions we all need help with.

Having started Reboot in 2017 to provide professional therapy and counseling, I had had numerous conversations with the therapists on these topics. And I often wondered if there was a way to reach out to those who do not walk into therapy rooms.

Friends would often ask, "what is therapy?" and I would repeat a line Astha would use. Imagine it's raining outside and you want to have a good time, you fear you will get wet and fall ill. While the doctor will give you medication to feel better, the therapist will give you a raincoat to ensure you can enjoy yourself and protect yourself. One often confuses it as someone who lends us a patient listening, but in reality it is much more. They teach us new life skills which are required for us to thrive in the new context life has placed us in. Therapy helps us build new habits and let go of old ones.

From Astha

As a therapist, I have had the privilege of stepping into the stories of countless individuals—stories brimming with heartbreak, resilience, hope, and transformation. Each narrative is unique, yet they all share one common thread: the power of perspective. Over the years, I've witnessed how the way we tell our stories—whether to others or to ourselves—shapes not only how we see the world but also how we feel and live within it.

Flip the Story is born from these experiences - both personal and professional. It is a collection of moments, conversations, and reflections that have profoundly moved me, not just as a therapist, but as a human being. it has helped me understand more deeply what means to navigate life's complexities. These stories are not just about the clients I've worked with; they are about all of us—the struggles we face, the emotions we wrestle with, and the transformations we are capable of when we dare to see things differently.

Personally speaking, my inspiration for this book (and of many other things in my life) is my co-founder Saloni. Since 2017, Saloni, has been so much more than a collaborator—she has been my greatest inspiration and one of life's most extraordinary blessings. Her enthusiasm for life, her boundless creativity, and the passion she brings to everything she touches have profoundly shaped me and the work we do at Reboot Wellness. It is her belief in me that gave me the courage to co-write this book. In so many ways, this book reflects her spirit & her faith - she motivated us to turn some of the most profound conversations into this piece of love and labour.

I am deeply grateful to Stuti and Neha for the time, effort, and creativity they poured into this book. Their dedication not only enriched this project but also brought us closer as colleagues, revealing the truly remarkable individuals they are. The moments we spent discussing stories and shaping narratives were some of the most reflective and extraordinary experiences of this journey. I couldn't be more thankful to have had Stuti and Neha by our side, making this process as meaningful as the final product itself.

This book is an invitation to look inward and challenge the narratives that may be holding you back. It is a reminder that while we cannot always control what happens to us, we can choose how we respond, how we interpret, and how we move forward. By shifting our stories, we can unlock new ways of understanding ourselves, our relationships, and the world around us.

Our hope is that these stories inspire you to reflect on your own life, to find courage in vulnerability, and to see that even in the darkest chapters, there is room for light. Change begins not with the events we endure but with the meaning we give them.

From Astha and Saloni

Another way to look at it is to imagine stepping into a room filled with possibility, a place where you can shed judgment and explore the hidden corners of your mind. Therapy offers a safe space to witness the unfolding of your inner world, understand its complexities, and rewrite the stories that hold you back. We hope to evoke emotions with the stories you read, sparking a sense of recognition and perhaps even a flicker of hope. But what really happens in the therapy room? You'll find a compassionate therapist who listens attentively, becoming a source of support as you bounce ideas around. A good therapist will ask difficult and pointed questions urging you to reflect on the situation and your behavior. It's like having a conversation with someone who truly understands you, and who does not have the same blind spots, offering a fresh perspective that challenges and empowers you. This therapist isn't there to dictate solutions, but rather to guide you towards making your own informed decisions.

Therapy, in essence, is about taking that first courageous step to confront your inner struggles. It's a space to build the tools you need to navigate life's challenges, strengthen relationships, and ultimately, become the person you've always envisioned yourself to be.

This isn't easy. Often the one who needs therapy will hesitate, resist or sometimes not be aware that therapy exists. Concerned family and friends create a safe space and an intervention to support a hurting individual. There are several ways to create an intervention and while we can write a chapter on the same, we will share a personal story from Saloni's life.

Back in 2012 when I (SM) was introduced to therapy a dear friend of mine who saw me slip every week from bad to worse staged a thoughtful intervention. She asked me if I could find a therapist for her as she needed support. When I found a good therapist for her, she asked me if I would accompany her. When we reached the therapist's premises and waited for our appointment, she asked me if I would come inside as she wasn't sure she could do this alone. When she finished sharing she gently asked me if I wanted to share as well. Slowly bit by bit she ensured I was in the right hands. That was the gentlest way to express love without interfering.

Consider this book a soft intervention, a packaged version of that expedition, one that equips you with valuable tools for self-discovery and growth. It aspires to help you get closer to your emotions and develop the skills to navigate them with newfound confidence. While this book won't replace the valuable experience of therapy, it aims to offer a similar sense of supportive guidance, especially if therapy isn't currently an option for you.

We have picked a few emotions which are hard for some of us to deal with and have suggested a way to flip the story in our own heads? But why do we need to Flip the Story for ourselves?

As we navigate our way through this maze called life, the narrative in our head determines the quality of our experiences, shapes our personalities, and allows us to become the best version of ourselves. The stories we tell ourselves become motivation, fueling the pursuit of dreams. And in a world of constant change, we learn to adapt with a creative twist, fostering deeper connections and uncovering a higher purpose in our journey.

Eckhart Tolle describes it beautifully, "The voice in my head was a veil of negative self-talk. What I took to be my life was a narrative in my mind[1]."

Being able to manage these emotions is like having a map that helps us navigate through ups and downs with strength. Crucially, emotion regulation isn't synonymous with suppressing emotions; rather, it's about acknowledging their existence and responding in

1. https://www.youtube.com/watch?v=HHhEPUp5X_I

a manner aligned with personal goals and values. It's the skill of containing the storm brewing within, harnessing its energy rather than being swept away by its force. Picture a skilled navigator steering through tumultuous waters, finding balance amid chaos.

Why is this skill essential? Its significance resonates on various levels, each intricately woven into the fabric of daily life. Many individuals adept at emotional regulation often exhibit greater mental resilience, standing firm against stress, anxiety, and depression. By understanding their emotions and their triggers, they equip themselves with the tools needed to weather life's inevitable storms.

Managing emotions helps us build stronger relationships. When we get better at understanding and handling our feelings, we communicate more kindly and handle disagreements calmly, without letting emotions take over. Learning to manage our emotions is a key life skill. It's about becoming more self-aware, changing how we think about problems, and finding ways to relax. It encourages us to pay attention to our feelings without getting caught up in them, using practices like meditation to create a peaceful space in our minds where we can deal with emotions in a healthy way. Getting good at this means changing how we think, challenging old habits of thought, and being open to new ways of dealing with tough emotions. It's a personal journey that happens every day, through the choices we make, the support we seek, and the way we see challenges as chances to grow.

Flip The Story is an exploration into the art of reframing life's experiences, especially when it comes to the stories we tell ourselves. It's about taking the reins of one's own narrative and steering it toward empowerment and resilience to weather storms while also finding meaning and growth in the challenges before us.

As Ashwani, one of our peer coaches and inspiration behind beginning Reboot, often says, it is critical to learn to live life on life's terms in order to experience life in all its glory. And on this journey, we engage with a range of emotions—helpful and unhelpful, healthy and unhealthy, empowering and debilitating. The book doesn't shy away from the vast spectrum of emotions; instead, it serves as a guide, illuminating a path toward understanding and harnessing these emotions for personal growth. We established the practice of Reboot in 2017 and this book is built out of conversations with a group of practicing clinical therapists, well-versed in the intricate landscapes of human emotions, Flip The Story draws from the wisdom of therapeutic practices, offering insights and strategies gleaned from the therapy rooms.

In these therapy rooms, individuals learn the skills shared in this book—skills designed to help navigate life. Therapists have witnessed firsthand the transformational power of reframing, of flipping the script on the narratives that hold us captive. Through shared experiences and professional insights, we, at

Reboot, bring forth a treasure trove of tools to aid in the navigation of life's emotional rollercoaster.

The book has an emotion we each identify with – it meets us in our lives more than once and how we respond in that moment is what determines the quality of our lives. Is it possible for us to Flip the Story in our heads when we get uncomfortable?

It isn't easy to Flip The Story, we struggle, we react, we resist yet if we are aware we can attempt, for our own sakes, to redefine our narrative to find renewed positivity and purpose.

As we deep-dived into each emotion and discovered its flip side, it proved to be a mix of therapy, revelation, and fresh perspectives for us as well. At times, it unearthed emotions we hadn't fully dealt with, offering us a chance to view them through a new lens. Our discussions were enriched by the contrasting yet complementary insights of my mother, whose deep spirituality brought a unique depth to our explorations, and the skilled therapists at Reboot, who provided professional guidance. This blend of personal wisdom and professional expertise created a nurturing environment for us to delve into the complexities of each emotion.

Each chapter of Flip The Story is an invitation to delve deeper into an emotion. Also, a note of caution, borrowed wisdom can be vicious and these are learnings from our journey and the journeys of our clients. Take what you like and leave the rest. Feel free to find your

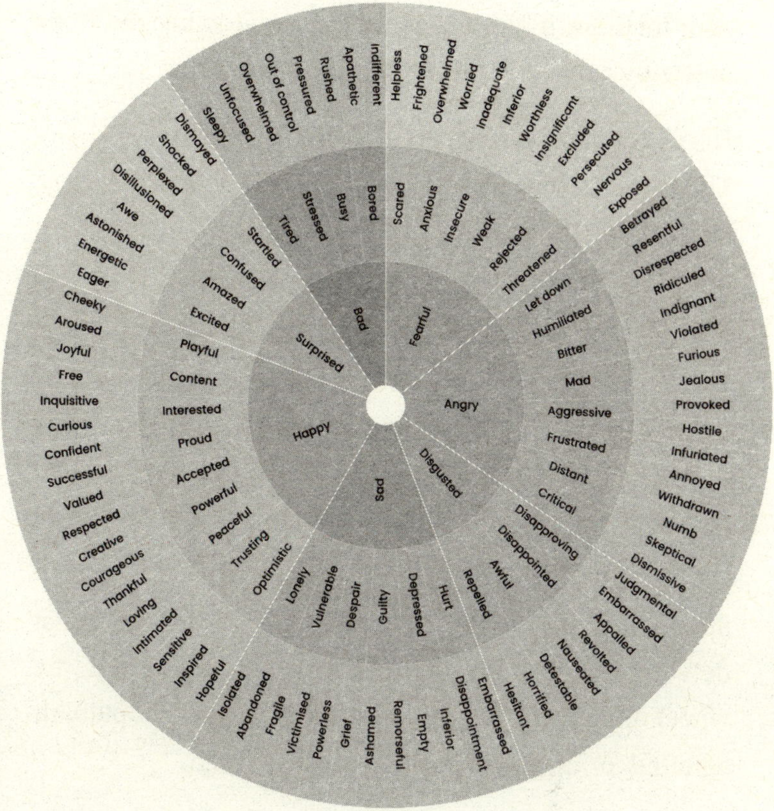

own flip words that may be more appropriate in your context.

We hope you find something in these pages that speaks to you, that helps you see your world a bit differently, and maybe even helps you change the way you interact with it. It's all about learning to dance in the rain, finding a bit of light in the dark, and maybe, just maybe, becoming the best version of ourselves along the way.

What you see in the earlier page is what is known as The Feelings Wheel. The Feelings Wheel is like a map for your feelings. It helps you understand your big emotions better by breaking them down into categories.

Here's how you can use it:

The Core: In the center are the big emotions like happy, sad, angry, and scared. This could be the starting point for the journey of your feelings. It shows the basic feelings everyone experiences, like happy, sad, mad (angry), and scared.

Deeper Dives: As you move outwards, the wheel gets more specific. It shows you different shades of each main emotion. For instance, under anger, you might find frustration, annoyance, or even resentment.

Super Specifics: The outermost layer has the most detailed feelings. Let's say you're feeling frustrated, the wheel might help you pinpoint if you're more impatient, agitated, or maybe even a little exasperated.

Anger

Curiosity

1

Exploring Anger

Navigating Life's Frustrations

> "*Anger is often what pain looks like when it shows itself in public.*"
>
> *– Krista Tippett*

Kavita, 28, seems to feel angry all the time these days, and today has been a hard day too. She didn't get the promotion she really wanted, and now, she can't find a parking spot in her neighbourhood. Her bad day at work and the hassle of driving home have made her feel really frustrated. She's starting to wonder if moving to Delhi was such a good idea after all. She is spent from all the arguing at work and cursing everyone on the road.

Kavita's mind is filled with so many thoughts and complaints that she's been holding in for too long. "Why do I always have to give in?" she thinks, feeling both angry and surprised. "Why can't anyone see how hard I try or the things I ignore in this neighbourhood?" These questions, though no one answers them, make her even more upset. She feels like no one in her neighborhood sees her or cares about what she needs.

After two futile rounds around the block, Kavita's pent-up frustration boils over. She takes a stand against her tyrannical neighborhood in the most dramatic fashion possible. Fed up, she parks her car right in the middle of the street and rings everyone's doorbell, loud and long. She refuses to be ignored this time.

As she waits, more determined than ever, her heart beats fast and she's ready to stand up for herself. Before anyone even comes outside, Kavita is sure about one thing: she's going to make them hear her out, no matter what it takes.

Doesn't this sound familiar? The feeling of injustice, the need to be heard, the raging discomfort and frustration that comes with it all?

Imagine being in Kavita's shoes – feeling exhausted, wronged, and desperate to protest. What do you think you might do or say in such a situation?

The first long ring is on the door of her neighbor Mira, who is 56 and lives alone. Mira likes her space and keeps a close watch over the parking spots in front of her house. She's used her defunct cars to claim this space, even though she cannot, and does not, drive them anymore. They are fixtures in the lane to ensure no one can use the space to park near her boundary wall. It's hers and she will do anything to stake her claim.

The next is 50-year-old Chetan, who is trying to enjoy a family dinner, but the parking mess outside is hard to ignore. He's known for keeping peace in the neighborhood, but tonight, he wishes people would solve their own problems. He just wants to have a good time with his family without any drama. He has eight parking spots in the stilt parking for his building but insists on parking his SUV right outside his house. His sweet-talking has allowed him to keep this extra spot. And why not, everyone else parks in front of their houses too.

The next ring is on Sanjay's door. Newly married a few weeks ago, his wife's new car needs a dedicated parking spot in this crowded lane. He needs to impress his new bride and has given her the most convenient spot in front of the house. Tonight, they have just settled in for a cozy, romantic evening after a delightful dinner together.

As the neighbors come out, Kavita doesn't hold back. She's loud and angry, and soon, everyone is shouting.

The tension has boiled over, and now they're all letting out their frustration. The fight escalates, with everyone blaming each other. They call each other names and don't listen to what anyone else has to say. It's a mess, and no one is backing down.

Anger is like that surge you feel when something really hits a nerve. It's not just about feeling mad; that your values or boundaries have been crossed and a feeling of injustice. I am not getting what I deserve or what is happening to me is not what I deserve. Another way to look at it could be to imagine it as a guard dog for your authenticity, urging you to stand up for what you believe in. It is the lack of vocabulary and the lack of articulating our feelings gracefully.

As they argue, it becomes clear that there's more to it than just parking spots. Kavita is upset about her job, about not being seen and the loneliness of a large city. Mira is fighting to claim the space she fears she will lose. Chetan wants a peaceful evening, and Sanjay is trying to enjoy the evening with his wife. They're all dealing with their own issues, and the parking problem was just the last straw. The argument doesn't get solved. Everyone goes back inside, angrier than before. The night is quiet again, but the tension is still there, thick in the air. The fight over parking has shown just how quickly things can turn bad when people are stressed and frustrated.

Anger always hides a story behind itself. It is our mind and body attempting to release many emotions in the form of one reaction – in a fight to change the circumstances.

Do the stories of Kavita, Mira, Chetan, and Sanjay sound familiar? Do their actions and reactions remind you of things you may have said or done, or those others may have said or done to you?

This whole fight really shines a light on anger and what it's actually about. Anger isn't the first feeling that pops up; it's what shows up after other feelings like frustration or being really stretched thin. When we have too much going on, we can't handle as much as we normally can. Anger can also come out when we take things too personally or think others are against us because of our own fears and worries.

Understanding that anger usually means there's something else going on underneath can help us deal with it better. It tells us to look deeper into why we're really upset. Maybe we're not just mad about what happened right now but about other things that have been bothering us for a while. Realizing this can help us get to the heart of the problem and start changing it, making things better for us.

Anger can often be an outlet for the powerlessness, injustice, and inadequacy we feel. It is a lot like an iceberg. What we see on the top is the expression but beneath all that fire are much deeper, very valid emotions.

Can you think of a time when you felt anger rising within you, as if you were a volcano about to erupt? When you only realized what you were truly feeling once that fire was extinguished?

Chetan is the one who understands the situation and is not quick to react. He reluctantly moves his car to make room for Kavita's and diffuses the situation. The neighbours have gone back to their homes, but the anger and the unresolved issues remain. It's a reminder of how quickly small problems can become big ones when tempers flare, triggering road rage and violence.

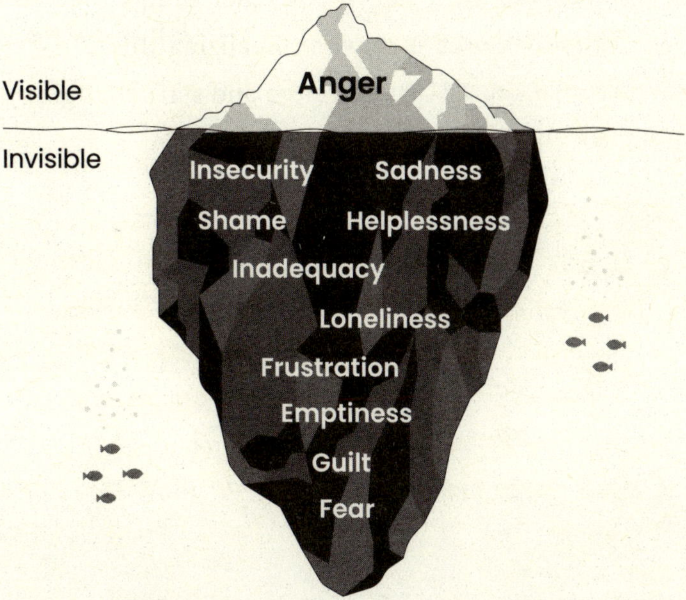

The Emotion Underneath Anger

Like all other feelings and emotions, anger too is real and valid. It wouldn't be fair to put it in a black box. Feelings are hardly black or white, good or bad – they just are. If there is one thing anger helps us with, it is understanding that there are unresolved thoughts, missed conversations, and in a lot of cases, a sense of isolation that are trying to make their presence known.

1. What are the early signs when you feel angry? Do you feel flushed, have sweaty hands, your mind goes blank, or thoughts get faster?

2. If you were Kavita, would you have to ring doorbells, literal or metaphorical, to assert yourself? Could there be another way?

3. How important is it for you to express your anger?

4. What would you do the next time you feel angry?

5. How would you want to look at your anger now?

Curiosity

The bridge from anger to understanding

> *Anger is a signal, and one worth listening to.*
>
> *– Harriet Lerner*

The sun peeked over the horizon, shedding light on what had been the battlefield of last night's neighborhood drama. It seemed almost comical how the orange glow washed over the silent witnesses – the trees, the benches, and the unsuspecting joggers of the park, oblivious to the verbal jousts that took place just hours ago. Chetan and Kavita, our protagonists from the evening's excitement, found themselves at the same crossroad, quite literally, in the park.

Chetan, who could give the Dalai Lama a run for his money in the zen department, offered a smile to Kavita. It was one of those smiles that said, "I've seen you at your Godzilla worst, but let's talk anyway." He's been watching Kavita's fuse getting shorter over the months, like a candle burning at both ends and figured a walk might just prevent another blow-up. So, there they were, walking side by side, stepping into the day's fresh start.

Kavita, driven by a mix of curiosity and last night's residual steam, asked Chetan how he keeps his cool when the rest of the world seems to be at each other's throats. Chetan decided to answer with a story that sounded like it belonged in one of those old, dusty fables.

It is a parable about a carpenter and a cobra. As a carpenter was closing his workshop for the day, without him realising, a black poisonous cobra slipped in. Hungry and in search of food, the cobra moved around the workshop and accidentally hit a saw, receiving a minor injury. The hangry cobra, driven by anger and a desire for revenge, bit the saw with full force, only to further hurt itself as its mouth started bleeding. Blinded by fury, the cobra attempted to strangle the saw, wrapping itself around the blades. The next morning, the carpenter found the dead cobra entangled in the saw. The tragic fate of the cobra was not caused by anyone else but was the direct result of its own anger. The moral? Anger can be as deadly, or even more deadly, to the bearer as it is to its intended target.

Anger is a bit more than a temper tantrum; it's like

a smoke alarm, telling you something's burning. But instead of throwing water on the electronics, Chetan suggested a more Sherlock Holmes approach – get curious. "Why am I ready to breathe fire?" is the starting clue.

"But pausing to play detective when you're about to go nuclear? That's like trying to thread a needle on a rollercoaster," Kavita pointed out.

Chetan agreed, "Oh, it's a beast, no doubt. Anger fries your brain. It's the lack of vocabulary to express yourself gracefully. But taking a moment to pause and be curious? That's your secret weapon."

He suggested practicing this Sherlock-ness in calmer moments, treating past instances of angry outbursts like cases gone cold which need to be revisited. This way, when anger shows up uninvited, you're better equipped to ask, "What's really happening here?" Meditation often helps us build this much-required skill at our own pace.

Giving Kavita a hopeful grin, he added, "Curiosity can flip anger on its head. It turns an automatic meltdown into a moment of choice."

So here is how we start being curious – we start by admitting to ourselves that we are angry. That we can't simply wish it away, but what we can do is acknowledge the feeling. The next step, of course, is to be curious about where the anger could be coming from.

Get a pen and paper and ask yourself –

What made me notice that I'm angry right now, what were the signs?

Is there something deeper that is pushing me to act out in this way?

Could I acknowledge that I'm angry, feel it, and think of helpful ways to resolve the feelings underlying my anger?

As they meandered through the park, blending tales of cobras and carpenters with musings on anger, curiosity, and the human condition, it felt like they were piecing together a map for navigating the tumultuous ocean of emotion. They parted ways with a lot to think about, especially about how curiosity isn't just an antidote to anger; it's a bridge to understanding – ourselves, and each other.

And just like that, Chetan and Kavita's morning walk transformed into a lesson in life itself – that curiosity might just be the most underrated superhero skill we all have, capable of turning reactions into responses and opening up that fleeting chance for much-needed connection, and maybe, just a bit of laughter at the absurdity of it all. And here lies the solution – talk it out.

1. Can you list people who you can confidently go up to and say – I am really angry today, and I want to tell you why and what is making me angry? Do we have such people in our lives?

2. What makes it easier for you to talk about your feelings instead of acting out in anger? Is there something you need from the other person in that moment to make you feel comfortable sharing your feelings?

3. Speak with anger and with curiosity – in different tones – say it aloud. Eg. 'What made you take this decision?'

4. If you deal with anger often, try using a Grounding Object. Keep a physical object handy that grounds you—something tactile that helps center your focus.

5. **Exit Strategy:** Identify a way to step away from a situation causing anger, allowing space for reflection.

Loneliness

Vulnerability

2

Loneliness

The Paradox of Our Connected World

> “*Loneliness is not lack of company, loneliness is lack of purpose.*”
>
> – ***Guillermo Maldonado***

Pankaj and Anita sat with hot coffee in their hands in a lovely coffee shop. A work acquaintance who had become a friend over the years, this young woman was very popular and much loved. She always had a warm smile, insights, a problem-solving mind, a large network, and an open heart that was always ready to help. She said gently, “I feel lonely!”

The admission hung in the air between them, stark against the backdrop of the bustling café, filled with the chatter and the clinking of cups. Her confession was a jarring contrast to her public persona. “I'm always surrounded by people," she continued, her voice barely above a whisper as if sharing a well-guarded secret. "But it feels like they're there for the version of me that helps, advises, and supports. It's like they're drawn to the light I emit, yet none are willing to stay and warm themselves by it."

Despite her extensive network, personal connections which went beyond superficial interactions were rare. Her openness and generosity, it seemed, had paradoxically built a wall around her; people didn't see her as someone who might also need support and companionship.

"It's as if I'm standing in a room full of people, yet the silence is overwhelming," she said. "Everyone sees me, but nobody really looks. They hear me, but they don't listen. It's lonely, being visible but not seen."

Loneliness is often used as a synonym for being alone. Being alone could refer to a space where you're without other people's physical presence. It can be a neutral experience, or it can come in the form of solitude. However, loneliness goes deeper than that. At the foundation of it, it is a feeling of isolation, disconnection, and a lack of meaningful connection with others.

The irony was not lost on Pankaj. Here was someone who epitomized connection and warmth, yet felt profoundly alone. It was a poignant reminder that loneliness does not discriminate; it can seep into the lives of even the most sociable and loved individuals. In sharing her vulnerability, she had opened a door for both of them to confront their own isolations, to recognise that beneath the façades of competence and cheerfulness we all wear, lies a fundamental need for connection, understanding, and acceptance.

In an era where technology has bridged vast distances, making it possible to connect with a click or a tap, loneliness remains a pervasive and profound experience. Despite the digital tools that keep us together, many of us find ourselves adrift in a sea of connectivity, surrounded yet isolated. This paradox highlights a fundamental truth: physical proximity and digital connectivity don't necessarily fulfill our deep-seated need for meaningful connection. Loneliness is perceived social isolation, our motivation to connect with people, however, it often takes us into a downward spiral where we become hypervigilant of our environment, not trusting it leading us to more negative displays of social interactions that further enhances our experience of feeling lonely. It's a catch 22. Because I'm feeling lonely, I'm more conscious, more aware of myself, not confident, possibly of who I am, or who I can trust. This further adds to my experience of feeling lonely. We're like sailors in our individual lifeboats, navigating a vast digital ocean, close enough to see each other but too far to touch.

Our epidemic of loneliness, says the U.S. Surgeon General's Advisory on the Healing Effects of Social Connection and Community,[2] is far more than just a bad feeling—it harms both individual and societal health. It is associated with a greater risk of cardiovascular disease, dementia, stroke, depression, anxiety, and premature death. The mortality impact of being socially disconnected is similar to that caused by smoking up to 15 cigarettes a day, and even greater than that associated with obesity and physical inactivity. And the harmful consequences of a society that lacks social connection can be felt in our schools, workplaces, and civic organizations, where performance, productivity, and engagement are diminished.

---

2. https://www.hhs.gov/sites/default/files/surgeon-general-social-connection-advisory.pdf

Loneliness doesn't discriminate; it can envelop anyone, regardless of age, social status, or relationship status. It's a universal feeling, akin to love or joy, yet it often dwells in the shadows of our lives, unacknowledged and hidden. From words we've held back to the vulnerability we've suppressed, and the connections we've longed for but not found. It's the echo of an empty house, the silence amidst a crowd, the mask we wear to navigate superficial social interactions. At its core, loneliness stems from a sense of social deficiency—a gap between the relationships we have and those we yearn for. It reflects a lack of deep, meaningful connections, a craving for someone to truly understand us and to share that understanding in return.

This longing for connection, for someone to recognise and appreciate our quirks and passions, is a basic human need. Yet, factors like fear, self-doubt, and life experiences that strain our bonds can intensify this sense of isolation. Additionally, the challenge of finding like-minded individuals with whom we can share genuine, heartfelt conversations contributes to our loneliness.

The idea of loneliness is derived from our need for attachment. From the moment we are born, the way we attach to a caregiver and as we grow up to other individuals in our lives.; shapes and forms who we are. It allows us to be socially integrated and feel worthy. Going deeper into our attachments and the need for the same allows us to understand that the vulnerability of being human lies in the quality and quantity of connections that human beings are able to form. This viability helps us regulate ourselves or emotions or thoughts makes us feel supported and hence helps us manage our fears and anxiety. I am not alone in this world. There are people who understand me. My existence has value and worth. these are some important components that attachments help us overcome, and what loneliness can destroy

There are times in our life where one would only expect joy and connection but those moments for some of us can feel disconnected and hence difficult for our mind to process. These are often periods of transition and growth – mothers on maternity leave, a young student who moves out of their parents' home, our first job in a new city, death of a loved one.

Recognising loneliness in ourselves and others requires introspection and honesty. Have we filled our lives with distractions, mistaking busyness for genuine connection? Do we truly feel safe and free to be ourselves with another? Are we surrounded by people, yet lonely within ourselves? This acknowledgment of loss comes with a sense of anxiety and fear, most of all the fear of being rejected, and the mind gets so consumed with unfulfilled social experiences that it fears feeling genuine connection. And that is the vicious cycle, we need to break. The question is, can we do this by ourselves? As human beings, do we have the bandwidth, the courage, the tools and skills to truly face who we are and step out of feeling lonely? Can we truly make ourselves feel safe by others when we are feeling so unsafe from within?

1. Have you ever felt lonely in a crowded room? Why do you think this happens?

2. When loneliness strikes do you seek a physical presence to fill the void? (Do you want to be with someone? Do you hide behind your phone and social media?)

3. How does loneliness manifest itself in your life (e.g., tearfulness, social withdrawal, difficulty concentrating)?

4. Do you find yourself seeking out distractions to avoid feeling lonely? If so, what are these distractions?

5. What fears or anxieties might be preventing you from forming deeper connections with others?

Vulnerability

A Bridge to Connection

> *Being vulnerable is the only way to allow your heart to feel true pleasure.*
>
> *– Bob Marley*

In the previous chapter, we tiptoed through the quiet rooms of our lives, peeking behind the curtains of busyness and solitude. We asked ourselves some pretty hard questions: Are we mistaking the hustle and bustle for real, soul-nourishing company? Can we truly kick off our shoes, throw our feet up on the coffee table, and be our unfiltered selves with someone? Or are we just actors in a crowded scene, feeling more alone than ever in our packed schedules?

To begin with you need to be aware that you are not broken when you feel lonely. It's only a signal from your body. Would you judge yourself when you feel thirsty? Or would you just grab a glass of water? Would you reprimand yourself when you feel hungry? Or would you just make yourself a snack? Loneliness is a signal from our body that we need connection.

The encounter in the coffee shop was a reminder that reaching out can sometimes be the bridge to finding solace and companionship. Leadership is a lonely job and Anita was facing stress from multiple fronts - but mostly her own expectations of herself. She was wise enough to understand that loneliness wasn't the enemy and took the opportunity to address her emotions - which isn't easy! But what might have helped the process was this little connection they shared.

Connection, in its purest form, is the invisible thread that binds us all together, not just with those in our immediate vicinity but with the world at large. It's the warmth we seek on a cold night and the light guiding us through our darkest moments. Shared laughter, silent understanding, the comfort of presence, and sometimes simply sharing not just our playlists but our deepest fears and wildest dreams.

Connection manifests in various forms, each significant in its own right. Emotional connections provide a shoulder to lean on, intellectual ones spark discussions that fuel the mind, spiritual connections offer solace in shared beliefs, and social connections weave us into the fabric of the community. Each form enriches our lives and the interactions define our existence. However, at the core of all connections lies the most crucial one: the connection with oneself. It's in the quiet moments alone that we confront our true selves, our values, and our aspirations. This inner dialogue shapes our actions, aligns our purpose, and grounds us. When this foundation is strong, it radiates outward, influencing every relationship we form.

Sometimes we place the entire burden of connection on very few people in our lives - spouses, siblings, parents, or some close friends. When they are unavailable or unable to be there for us, it leads to disappointment. We know from basic physics that a highly concentrated force will result in very high pressure, which in human relationships can be very unhealthy. To grow and thrive as individuals, you need to distribute this need or requirement, and in psychology there is a simple theory of concentric circles to understand our need for connection.

To understand this, imagine your social world as a series of concentric circles, each representing different levels of connection. The innermost circle is the connection one has with oneself - our values and our actions have to align for us to feel connected and grounded. It's like wearing shoes that don't fit; no matter how beautiful they are, you'll end up feeling uncomfortable. When your actions and values are in sync, you walk through life with a sense of purpose and integrity. This alignment brings a deep sense of connection to who you truly are, making you feel grounded and centered, even when the world around you is in chaos.

Next are your closest relationships—your core group. Family members, partners, and best friends. These are the people who know you deeply, who see beyond the façade we often present to the world. Your connection with them is marked by unconditional love, trust, and a profound understanding that doesn't need words to communicate. Typically, an individual has five people in this circle, however, research shows changes in our social structure, and hyper-dependence on social media has gone down to one person for many of us. An over-dependence on one individual becomes unhealthy.

This is followed by our inner circle. Just beyond our core group are close friends and confidants, those with whom you share significant parts of your life. These relationships are built on shared interests, mutual respect, and a sense of camaraderie. While the connection might not be as deep as with your core group, it's still marked by a strong sense of support and belonging. Mentors and 1–2 colleagues at work, old friends who grew up and have been around, and relatives we rely on and trust often make our inner circle.

Beyond the inner circle are acquaintances and these include colleagues, neighbors, and social connections. These relationships might not delve into the depths of your personal life, but they add richness and diversity to your social landscape. They're the ones you share friendly conversations with, exchange smiles, and occasionally, share moments that can blossom into deeper friendships. These are the folks you meet at a party, the ones who have interesting banter and gossip.

Then there are strangers, who are also important. Even fleeting interactions with strangers can spark a sense of connection, reminding us of our shared humanity. A smile, a kind gesture, or a brief exchange of words could sometimes leave a lasting impression, highlighting the potential for deep connections in unexpected places.

Part of being human is interdependence because we evolved to live in a tribe. We need people, relationships, looking out for each other, banding together – we need each other. We like to solve each other's problems, be useful, and lean on each other when we need to. For this, we need to find our tribe – the school group, the college friends, the friends of friends who you love hanging out with, the office bunch, or the alumni from your previous office who love to reminisce about old times, the spiritual group, the religious folks, the fitness enthusiasts, the choice is yours. We also need to remember that the nature of our current connections, as life moves on, changes. Our concentric circles and those we place in them will change after major life events be it marriage, divorce, a change of job, moving cities, and death to name a few.

When we feel disconnected and we feel an aching pain to find a connection, it helps to do something for someone. Anyone. Small acts of service help make connections and that is critical to our survival. It could be a hug to our siblings or partner, calling an old friend

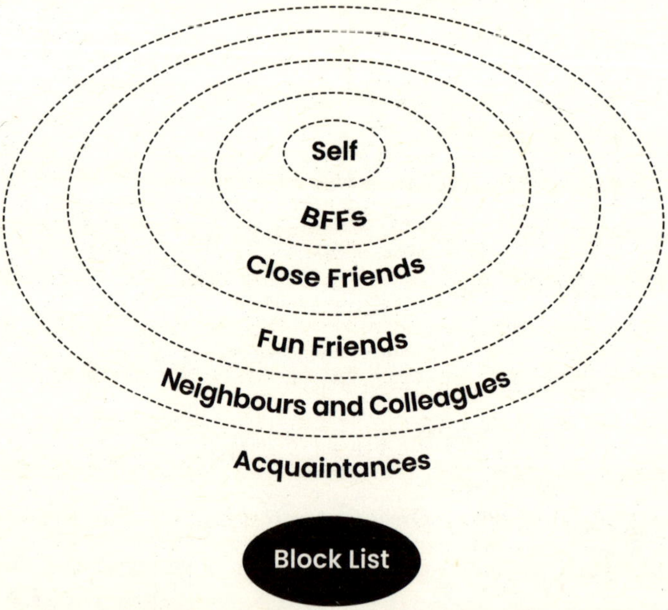

Concentric Circle of Connections

to check on them, a coffee with an acquaintance who we wish to know better, a small dessert for our neighbour, just giving something to drink to the cop down the street or handing a young kid a chocolate, participating in the community to volunteer or feeding a stray animal. In the presence of connection, loneliness withers like grass, and as the author of Lost Connection, Johan Hari sums it up, *"As the garden begins to bloom, we begin to bloom."*

Decades of research across disciplines such as political science, economics, sociology, behavioural science, and public health, among others, have examined the relationship between group social connection and population health and well-being. These studies establish that social connection is vital not only to our individual physical, mental, and emotional health, but also to the health and well-being of our communities.

1. One thing that you would build as a ritual to improve your connection with yourself

2. Who would you want to connect with or improve your connection with? How would you connect with them?

3. How can you be more authentic and vulnerable in your interactions with others? How can you challenge your fear of being vulnerable in order to build stronger connections?

4. How can you identify and nurture the meaningful connections in your life?

5. How can you take an active role in finding the connections you crave?

Resentment

Acknowledgment

3

Unpacking Resentment

The Uninvited Guest in Life's Journey

> "*Resentment is like drinking poison and then hoping it will kill your enemies.*"
>
> *– Nelson Mandela*

Gauri and Kabir met at their first job, a bustling media company filled with the energy of young professionals eager to make their mark. They were both fresh out of college, excited about their careers and even more excited about life. Gauri's infectious laughter and Kabir's quick wit made them fast friends. Shared lunches turned into long evening walks, and before they knew it, they were deeply in love.

Their relationship blossomed quickly. Kabir proposed on a rainy evening, under the very tree where they had their first kiss. Their wedding was a beautiful blend of their cultures, a celebration of their love and the hopeful future they saw together. They dreamt of a life filled with adventure, success, and a family.

For the next ten years, Gauri and Kabir built a life many would envy. They bought a beautiful home and were blessed with two children who brought endless joy and laughter into their lives. Kabir was a loving husband and father, always there to support and care for his family. Gauri managed the household with grace, balancing her career and her role as a mother.

Their home was filled with love and happiness. Family dinners, weekend outings, and bedtime stories were the norm. They were a team, facing life's challenges together and celebrating its joys with equal fervor.

One day, Gauri felt a sharp pain in her hands. She brushed it off initially, attributing it to the fatigue of juggling work and home. But the pain persisted, and soon, she found it difficult to move her fingers. Concerned, she visited a doctor. After months of tests and consultations, Gauri was diagnosed with an autoimmune condition.

The news hit them hard. They scoured the internet, trying to understand the condition and what it meant for their future. They made necessary lifestyle changes, hoping to manage Gauri's health better. However, her condition deteriorated over the next year, and the medication grew stronger, bringing with it a slew of side effects.

Throughout this challenging time, Kabir was a pillar of strength. He took charge of the household, ensuring Gauri had everything she needed. He managed the kids' schedules, cooked meals, and maintained their home. He was ever-loving and supportive, putting Gauri's needs above his own. Kabir took pride in being the provider, the one who held everything together.

But as Gauri's condition became more demanding, Kabir's needs took a back seat. His dreams, his hobbies, even his simple desire for a quiet evening became secondary to the needs of his wife and children. Kabir's life revolved around managing Gauri's health and keeping the family afloat.

For years, Kabir managed to suppress his feelings. He told himself that it was the noble thing to do, to fulfill his duty, his responsibility as a husband and father. This suppression is what helped him carry on even though the situation was challenging. But eventually, he couldn't keep it in and resentment began to creep in. It started as a faint whisper, a fleeting thought, but over time, it grew louder.

Resentment is not the same as anger. In fact, it is a multilayered, complex reaction to difficult circumstances – a mix of disappointment, understanding, and wanting to be realistic. While we may understand the circumstances intellectually, our mind still wants to fulfill its inner needs, which leaves us feeling bitter and unsatisfied.

Friends stopped inviting them to social gatherings, knowing Gauri's condition made it hard for them to attend. Kabir missed the camaraderie and felt increasingly isolated. When he couldn't attend his son's soccer match because Gauri had a medical emergency, Kabir saw the disappointment in his son's eyes and felt a stab of resentment towards the situation. It was as if the universe had conspired to keep him tethered to a life he hadn't planned for, a life where his needs were perpetually on hold.

Kabir would often find himself feeling frustrated over small things. He'd watch Gauri struggle with simple tasks, his heart aching for her, but also feeling a pang of resentment that their life had become so difficult.

When he saw other couples enjoying carefree lives, the emotion tugged at him harder. He struggled with it, not knowing what to call it let alone address it.

One evening, after a particularly grueling day at work and an even tougher evening at home, Kabir felt the weight of his emotion heavier than usual. Gauri needed help with her medication, the kids were fighting, and the house was a mess. As he rushed to meet everyone's needs, he felt a surge of anger. Why did everything always fall on him? Why couldn't he have a moment of peace? This anger had a tone of sadness, even empathy, but the disappointed voice was so loud that it was impossible to ignore.

He would often find himself annoyed with these unpleasant feelings. He would talk to them, saying, "It's a shit-hit-the-fan kind of day, I don't need you here. Bugger off!"

The resentment grew quietly, like a weed in a garden, unnoticed until it had taken firm root. He remembered the times he had to decline a promotion because the new role required travel, and he couldn't leave Gauri and the kids behind. Each time he saw his colleagues advance in their careers, resentment flared up, and it became harder and harder to act rational and calm.

Resentment often makes it hard to stop the surge of mixed emotions- the unresolved grief, extremely high expectations, and unfulfilled dreams. It carries a desire for justice, with the backdrop of intellectual understanding. It can be a heavy conflict that makes it extremely difficult to find closure.

Kabir spent hours planning Gauri's birthday, hoping to lift her spirits. But when the day arrived, Gauri was too ill to celebrate. Her gratitude was genuine but brief, leaving Kabir feeling underappreciated. It was in these moments that resentment wrapped itself around his heart a little tighter. Gauri, absorbed in her own pain and struggles, didn't notice Kabir's growing resentment. She couldn't see the exhaustion in his eyes, the weariness in his movements. She was grateful for his support but unaware of the emotional toll it was taking on him.

When we are resentful, we often find ourselves stuck in loops of blame, either actively or passively, and sure enough,

that is what is reciprocated to us. However, every feeling has a meaning behind it, and so does resentment- to protect us from unanticipated disappointment. In a situation like this, we learn to expect disappointment, and this has the potential to become a self-fulfilling prophecy. The resolution to resentment lies in addressing the function and impact of the feeling, and recognising and stating our needs.

Kabir's resentment wasn't born out of a lack of love for Gauri or their children. It stemmed from the unrelenting demands of their situation and the gradual erasure of his own needs and desires. His boundaries were stretched, taking away from the genuineness and authenticity of the relationship. He loved Gauri deeply, but the constant caregiving, the endless sacrifices, and the loss of his own identity were taking their toll. This resentment, left unaddressed, threatened to overshadow the love and dedication that had been the foundation of their relationship.

1. What came to your mind as you read Gauri and Kabir's story of resentment? Was it a person, a situation, a relationship, or something else?

2. Is the feeling in your body associated with thoughts of resentment pleasant or unpleasant? How does it manifest physically and emotionally?

3. Reflect on a specific incident or situation that triggered resentment in your life. What were the circumstances, and how did you initially react to it?

4. Addressing resentment is hard, even if it is about accepting it to our own selves. What feelings do you associate with resentment? What feelings sound or feel like resentment?

5. Can you recall a time when you successfully managed or released feelings of resentment? What strategies or practices did you find most effective in this process?

Acknowledgment

The Healing Balm for Resentment

> *Acknowledgment is the first step in healing and growth. It is the bridge between resentment and peace.*
>
> *– Unknown*

It was that time of year again—appraisals at work. Kabir had prioritized his family over his career for the last few years, and as a result, the radio station got a new Station Head. Kabir would now report to him. The promotion that should have been his was given to someone else, and it hurt deeply. Despite his internal turmoil, Kabir introduced the new boss to the organiation, masking his raging emotions with humour.

"Meet our new Station Head," Kabir announced with a forced smile. "He's the guy who gets to handle all the complaints now, so if your coffee is too cold or your chair is too squeaky, you know where to go!"

While everyone laughed, Kabir felt a pang of bitterness. He had worked hard for this role, and now he was left to introduce the person who had taken his place. The resentment simmered beneath his cheerful facade. Kabir felt a deep pang of disappointment. This should have been his promotion, his moment of recognition. The sacrifice for his family felt heavier than ever.

Before winding down for the day, with a head full of shattered dreams, Kabir was visibly distraught. Dev, a younger colleague and a friend asked Kabir, "Care for a drink?" Without a thought Kabir said, "Many!"

Dev had seen Kabir change over the last few years and he knew from his own experience that what was required was a gentle intervention. As they walked into the bar, Dev was talking about his struggles at home and mentioned that he had been attending a Support Group for Men to deal with the challenges and changes in his life. Kabir caught bits and pieces of Dev's story as the music in the bar drowned out his voice.

Over beer and banter, Dev shared more about the group and how it had helped him grow in a positive and healthy way. Kabir had never heard of men sitting in a group talking about emotions and couldn't quite wrap his head around it.

"So, what do you guys actually talk about?" Kabir asked, leaning in to hear better.

"Everything," Dev replied. "From work stress to family issues. It's about being honest with our feelings and supporting each other. It's kind of like therapy, but in a group setting."

"Is it... awkward?" Kabir asked, still skeptical.

"At first, yeah," Dev admitted. "But you get used to it. And honestly, it's been a lifesaver. It's like a weight off your shoulders, knowing you're not alone. Once we learn to regulate our emotions vs control our emotions, we react less and better. It just helps me get out of my head and reduces stress and loneliness."

Kabir picked his pint and winked, "This does the same!" but he knew that there was a fine line between magic and tragic and his life was leaning towards the latter, should he give this group a shot? He could no longer just sink another drink and carry one, he needed some help.

Intrigued by Dev's experience, Kabir decided to give the support group a try. The first meeting felt strange. Sitting in a circle with other men, sharing personal stories, wasn't something he was used to. But as he listened to others speak about their struggles and triumphs, Kabir began to feel a sense of connection.

When it was his turn to speak, Kabir hesitated but then opened up. "I've been dealing with a lot at home. My wife has a serious health condition, and it's been tough balancing everything. I guess... I just feel overwhelmed and... resentful sometimes."

The group listened without judgment. Some nodded in understanding, others shared similar experiences. For the first time in a long while, Kabir felt seen and heard.

Through the support group, Kabir learned the importance of acknowledgement. He began recognising his mixed feelings of resentment and accepting them without guilt. He acknowledged the sacrifices he had made and the frustration he felt about his career.

Judith W. Umlas, author and Senior Vice President of the International Institute for Learning, outlined the 5 Cs of acknowledgement in her book 'The Power of Acknowledgement'. Adapting her model to acknowledgement to the current context, this may be how we use the 5 Cs:

Consciousness: Noticing your needs and feelings of dissatisfaction.

Choice: Making the choice to respect your feelings and act on them.

Courage: Recognising that it is important to convey your needs, and deciding the right time, tone, and way of conveying them.

Communication: The process of efficiently conveying your needs to the other to reach a resolution.

Commitment: **Persevering in the process of resolving your feelings of resentment.**

Kabir also realized the importance of communicating his feelings to Gauri. One evening, after the kids were in bed, he sat down with her and opened up.

"Gauri, I need to share something important," he began. "I've been feeling overwhelmed and resentful. It's not because of you, but because I've neglected my own needs. I want us to find a better balance."

Gauri listened, her eyes filling with tears. She hadn't realized the extent of Kabir's struggles. His acknowledgment allowed her to empathize with him and understand his perspective.

With acknowledgment came the realization that changes were needed. Kabir and Gauri decided to make adjustments in their lives. They hired a full-time caregiver to help with Gauri's needs, giving Kabir some much-needed respite. Kabir also carved out time for his hobbies and interests, rediscovering activities that brought him joy.

They restructured household responsibilities over the next one year, involving the kids in age-appropriate chores. This not only eased Kabir's burden but also taught their children valuable life skills. It was not easy but everyone understood their part and took responsibility.

As Kabir continued to practice acknowledgment, he noticed a significant change. The resentment that once weighed him down began to lift. He felt lighter, more connected to Gauri and the kids, and more at peace with himself.

As human beings, we can compromise on many things, except those that we consider truly valuable to us. The path to acknowledgement begins with valuing our own self and our values while balancing responsibilities. Identifying our values and trying to inculcate them into our lives even in a difficult situation can help us cope with challenging circumstances.

Acknowledgment is not as much about changing the situations as it is about changing the way we respond to it- to feel capable of regulating it. Kabir acknowledging his needs did not eliminate the challenges or change the situation, but it equipped him with the tools to handle them better. By recognising and accepting his feelings, he could address them constructively rather than letting them fester.

Kabir learned that acknowledgment was the key to overcoming resentment. By facing his feelings and communicating openly with Gauri, he found a way to balance his needs with those of his family. The love and dedication that had always been the foundation of their relationship grew stronger, allowing them to face life's challenges with empathy and understanding.

Acknowledgment transformed their story from one of hidden resentment to one of mutual support and resilience. It was a journey of learning and growth that helped him embrace the sweetness of love and the bitterness of life.

1. Can we love and resent someone at the same time?

2. Is it possible to fix resentment, especially in our relationships?

3. How did you banish the bitterness that you may have felt towards someone or a situation?

4. Can you think of a time when you effectively communicated what you were feeling to the person you wanted to? How did it feel? How did it impact the relationship?

5. Acknowledgement of difficult circumstances is tough but needed. Would you like to acknowledge something in your life and relieve yourself from the suppression?

Dependency

Interdependence

4

Dependency

Navigating Mixed Signals

> *Dependence on others for your own happiness is the most foolish thing to do.*
>
> *– Unknown*

Utkarsh and Sheena had known each other since their early school days. Their friendship began on the first day of middle school when a shy new student, 13-year-old Utkarsh, struggling with his new environment, found a friend in Sheena. Utkarsh was an introverted, thoughtful individual who found solace in routines and familiar surroundings. His childhood was marked by a constant search for stability, as his parents' demanding careers and hectic jobs often left him feeling lonely. Sheena had been in this school since nursery. She was outgoing, confident, and always ready with a smile. Her vibrant personality and unwavering support provided him with a sense of belonging in this new, unknown city and school.

Over time, their friendship deepened as Utkarsh and Sheena became inseparable. They learned new things together, each experience strengthening their bond. They taught each other to swim, initially floundering in the shallow end of the pool but soon mastering the freestyle stroke. Cycling became their shared adventure, with Utkarsh pushing Sheena to ride faster and her encouraging him to explore new terrains. Their first metro ride was a memorable event, filled with laughter and excitement as they navigated the city on their own.

As they grew older, their adventures took on new dimensions. They learned to drive together, spending countless hours in empty parking lots, perfecting parallel parking and hill starts. Sheena's confidence balanced Utkarsh's cautious approach, making them a perfect team. Their friendship flourished through these shared milestones, becoming a cornerstone in each other's lives. Every new skill they acquired, every challenge they faced, they did so together, building a foundation of trust and mutual support. Their bond was more than just companionship; it was a partnership that had seen them through the highs and lows of adolescence and early adulthood.

Over time, their friendship deepened. The childhood love and support developed a new meaning. Both of them felt an undeniable attraction towards each other. It was at this stage, as they started college, that their friendship evolved into a romantic relationship. They studied together, ate meals together, and shared their dreams and fears. Sheena was Utkarsh's rock, providing him with unwavering support during his bouts of self-doubt. Her validation made him feel empowered. Utkarsh was Sheena's safe space, where she could be vulnerable and honest without fear of judgment. Utkarsh became adept at reading her moods, offering support before she even asked for it. In many ways, they seemed perfectly aligned.

Sheena often struggled with late-night studies and appreciated Utkarsh offering to quiz her or help her understand difficult concepts. They made a pact to never study apart, their study sessions filled with snacks and supportive banter.

During exams, Utkarsh would panic if Sheena wasn't there to study with him. Her presence calmed him, making him feel more confident. Without her, he felt his concentration wane. Sheena would often find him in a fluster, gently guiding him back to focus with her calm demeanor.

Utkarsh avoided social gatherings unless Sheena accompanied him. He felt out of place in crowds without her by his side. Sheena enjoyed meeting new people, and always made sure to include him, holding his hand through every party and gathering. It made her heart warm to introduce Utkarsh to people as her partner. The people they would meet would often look at them in admiration- secretly hoping they would find love like theirs one day. However, when Utkarsh was not interested in attending an event, Sheena would often turn down invitations, not wanting him to feel left out and neglected. Her friends joked about their inseparability- they seemed to complement each other perfectly.

When Utkarsh had a particularly bad day, Sheena's voice would console him, and together they would arrive at solutions. Sharing his worries with her became his way of coping with them, Sheena's presence would calm him like nothing else would.

While most of us have that one person who is a safe space for us, where we can talk, share, and be understood, sometimes the boundaries can get blurred. The comfort that Utkarsh felt with Sheena was so effective in calming him, that he never developed his own resources to cope with life and its challenges. His trouble regulating his emotions or forming other

connections was never challenged as long as Sheena was around. For Sheena, too, this meant being overly responsible and constantly helping Utkarsh through his difficult feelings.

Such circular relationships form the codependence cycle- where one partner needs the other partner, who in turn feels overly responsible for providing that support. The dysfunctionality gets highlighted with Utkarsh not being able to find satisfaction or happiness outside of the relationship.

Academically gifted, Utkarsh excelled in computer science, dreaming of a career that would allow him to innovate and solve complex problems. His meticulous nature and analytical mind earned him a top spot in his class, leading to several job offers from prestigious companies.

As their college years came to an end, a world of opportunities seemed to open up for both Utkarsh and Sheena. Sheena's opportunity to study abroad on a scholarship came first, filling her with excitement. They were both proud and excited for each other.

Shortly after, Utkarsh received an equally prestigious offer in an up-and-coming startup in a different city within the country, aligning perfectly with his career aspirations. They were both proud and excited for each other.

This turn of events brought up many feelings for both of them. The prospect of being separated from Sheena filled Utkarsh with anxiety and fear. Sheena, too, was conflicted and sad. Their relationship was at a crossroads, torn between being together versus exploring the potential for things that they had worked so hard for. A long-distance relationship? Giving up on the idea of moving in together? This new stage in life posed new questions, a lot of confusion, and a feeling of uncertainty that neither of them had felt with each other before. They were both struggling, being pulled in opposite directions. They had to decide whether to pursue their careers separately or try to maintain a long-distance relationship. The idea of moving together was enticing but posed its own set of challenges, as it would mean one of them compromising on their dream.

Feeling a sense of anxiety or fear in situations that are unpredictable or pose a major challenge is completely

understandable. It is only human to be taken aback by new circumstances. The more critical decisions of our lives often bring us face to face with the complexity of our emotions and give rise to many internal conflicts. However, the nature of life is such that these situations do come up, and it is our inescapable responsibility to learn to hold ourselves and feel what we are feeling – though it may feel like the most difficult task of our lives.

Utkarsh didn't voice it, but he silently hoped Sheena would choose to follow him to the new city, just as she had always stood by him. The thought of her moving abroad, thousands of miles away from him, filled him with dread. He felt a profound sense of betrayal at the idea that Sheena would actually take up this opportunity, convinced that their bond would take priority over any educational or career opportunity. His dependence on Sheena was almost robbing him of seeing the bigger picture and their individual aspirations – the resistance to any change in their relationship dynamic was so strong that Utkarsh was even beginning to consider giving up his own coveted job opportunity.

This phase is revealing of dependence – emotional, social, and sometimes even physical – on one another. A dependence that was now becoming limiting.

In a relationship, when we are constantly dependent on our partner to pull us up, we risk burning them out and reducing our shared capability to take care of ourselves. We also tend to have expectations that may not be practical and realistic- limiting ourselves and them. The reality of change triggers that deeply rooted fear of abandonment and questions our sense of safety.

As we start to constantly rely on others for our sense of safety, it leads to a loss of identity and individuality. We tend to attach our identity with that of another person in our life. The mind fears that unpredictable disruption would take that person away, hence robbing us of the feeling of security and comfort. This seems to pose a serious threat to our well-being.

On the other hand, Sheena viewed these new avenues as stepping stones to a wonderful future for both of them together. Though also sad, anxious, and equally dreading the change; she didn't share the same fears. She believed that their relationship would prove to be a source of strength in this fresh set of challenging circumstances. She knew they had the courage to pursue their dreams, while still preserving and growing in their relationship.

Their last few weeks together were marked by a profound sense of sadness and uncertainty. They clung to each other, fighting each moment and turning this beautiful relationship into a bitter battleground. Utkarsh's nights were restless, filled with anxiety about the future. Sheena, torn between her aspirations and her love for Utkarsh, grappled with guilt and hesitation.

Their conversations became a blend of reminiscing about their past and speculating about an uncertain future. The once vibrant and joyful relationship now bore the strain of looming separation. The emotional dependency that had once brought them closer now threatened to break them apart. As they discussed their future, the conversation quickly turned sour. Utkarsh couldn't hide his disappointment and anger – he felt Sheena was okay leaving him behind. "I can't believe you'd even consider moving so far away. Did you even once think about us?" he asked bitterly. Sheena, equally frustrated, retorted, "This is my dream, Utkarsh. I thought you of all people would understand that and support us. I have been applying to these universities for over a year. You knew this was coming!" Utkarsh felt abandoned, unable to fathom a life without Sheena's constant comforting presence, while Sheena was taken aback by the expectation of having to let go of her dream college for the sake of their relationship.

Utkarsh's reliance on Sheena for validation had always been a quiet undercurrent in their relationship. Without her, he felt his worth diminish, and the fear of losing that external validation intensified his sense of betrayal. Sheena, on the other hand, struggled with the realization that her self-worth had become deeply intertwined with Utkarsh's dependence on her. She began to question her own identity, feeling lost without the constant affirmation she provided him.

Their once harmonious partnership started to crack under the weight of their conflicting aspirations. Utkarsh's anxiety grew, making him clingier and more resentful, constantly questioning Sheena's commitment to their relationship. He became preoccupied with his unmet needs, failing to recognise that Sheena had needs and dreams too. This lack of accountability led to more arguments, each accusing the other of being selfish and inconsiderate. Sheena, feeling increasingly trapped and confused, began to pull away. She constantly felt Utkarsh's inability to support her ambitions. The joy and excitement that once characterized their bond were replaced by arguments and emotional exhaustion. Each felt the other was being selfish, leading to a cycle of blame and bitterness. This negative spiral left them both distraught and confused, their deep-rooted dependency now a source of pain rather than comfort.

Utkarsh felt he was not understood and that his needs were not met. He began to feel like Sheena was not in his corner as much as he had previously thought. His resentment grew as he felt Sheena had failed to meet his expectations, while Sheena struggled with the imbalance in their relationship, feeling burdened by Utkarsh's dependence on her for his emotional stability. The foundation of trust and support they had built over the years seemed to crumble, leaving them jaded and angry, struggling to reconcile their affection for each other with their individual dreams.

As Sheena boarded the plane, leaving Utkarsh behind, each of them carried a heavy heart filled with pain, hesitation, and unanswered questions. A friendship, understanding and reliance that once brought them together now seemed to tear them apart, leaving a void that neither knew how to fill.

Imagine you are walking with someone and at some point, you put your weight on that person. The person moves slightly and you lose your balance and fall down. This could be true in our relationships too. While we need all our relationships to help us walk the difficult parts of life, build a sense of safety and feel comforted, these relationships cannot be the only source of our safety. We need ourselves as much as we need others. Often, the fear attached to relationships makes them heavier to carry forward.

1. In what ways can emotional dependency impact personal growth and the dynamics of a relationship?

2. How can individuals balance their own aspirations and needs while maintaining a supportive relationship?

3. What steps can be taken to ensure that a relationship remains a source of strength rather than a limitation?

4. How can one develop a sense of self-worth and validation independently of a partner or relationship?

5. What strategies can help individuals navigate the fear of change or separation in relationships?

Interdependence

Redefining Connection

> *The strongest relationships are between two people who can live without each other but don't want to.*
>
> ***– Harriet Lerner***

Sheena was now in the US, immersed in the glittering world of New York City. The towering skyscrapers, bustling streets, and endless opportunities fascinated her, filling her days with a sense of adventure and excitement. She threw herself into her work, finding joy in the challenges and triumphs of her new role. The city that never sleeps matched her pace, and she began to thrive in an environment that was both demanding and exhilarating.

At the same time, Utkarsh felt a bitter sense of disconnection from Sheena. While he was immersed in his new life in Bangalore, the emptiness left by her absence gnawed at him daily. He thrived in his startup, receiving accolades and making new friends, but the happiness felt incomplete. He couldn't shake the feeling of unfairness that Sheena had left him behind to pursue her dreams abroad. Their calls were filled with longing and unspoken sadness, each trying to mask their pain for the sake of the other. Utkarsh often found himself reminiscing about their shared moments, feeling an emptiness that his work couldn't fill. Sheena, too, missed the comfort of Utkarsh's presence, the familiar reassurance that had always grounded her.

This feeling of heaviness and bitterness was gnawing at him and one of his new friends suggested that he go see a therapist. Utkarsh sat on the plush couch in the therapist's office, his posture rigid and his expression a mixture of sadness and frustration. The room was softly lit, creating a calming atmosphere, but he struggled to feel at ease.

Ms. Menon, his therapist, observed him with a compassionate expression. "Utkarsh, I can see you're carrying a lot of heavy emotions today. Would you like to tell me what has been going on for you?"

Utkarsh filled Ms. Menon in on his relationship history with Sheena, and the recent transition that they had been going through. As he started to address his feelings about Sheena leaving, he sighed deeply. "It's Sheena. I know I should be happy for her and her new opportunities, but I can't shake this feeling of being left behind. It's unfair that she left me when I needed her the most. I feel so disconnected from her, and it just... hurts."

Ms. Menon nodded; her eyes full of understanding. "It's perfectly natural to feel that way, Utkarsh. It sounds like you're dealing with a mix of many different emotions. These feelings are important to acknowledge. Can you describe what these emotions feel like for you?"

Utkarsh leaned back, closing his eyes for a moment. "It's like this constant ache in my chest. I feel abandoned, like she chose her dreams over me. And then I feel guilty for even thinking that because I know how important this opportunity is for her. I want her to be happy and achieve what she deserves, but I can't help it. I feel like she just left me, she left us, and everything that we built over the years."

Ms. Menon gave him a moment before speaking again. "Thank you for sharing that with me. It sounds like you're experiencing a deep sense of loss." "It is a loss and so much more," Utkarsh muttered softly with his eyes closed. Ms. Menon said: "I understand how you feel, Utkarsh. It's important to sit with these feelings, even though they're uncomfortable. Let's try to explore them a bit more. What is it about Sheena's departure that feels most painful to you?"

All feelings are natural. They are our response to life and circumstances. We can't 'unfeel' what we are feeling. However, the only way forward is by 'going through' these feelings – accepting that they exist.

Utkarsh opened his eyes, staring at the ceiling. "I guess it's because she was my constant. She was always there for me, and now she's not. I depended on her for so much, and now I feel like I'm floundering without her. I feel like I'm not enough on my own and I have no one."

Ms. Menon leaned forward slightly. "It's understandable to feel that way, especially when someone who has been such a significant part of your life is suddenly not physically present. You mentioned feeling like you're not enough on your own. Where do you think that thought comes from?"

Utkarsh frowned, thinking. "I guess... I've always relied on her, she was always there making me feel alive and happy. She was my rock, my support system. Without her, I feel lost. I don't trust myself to handle things as well. I guess I never really thought of myself beyond her presence and care."

Ms. Menon nodded thoughtfully. "It sounds like Sheena was a significant source of your self-worth and confidence. Let's consider this: what if this period without her presence is an opportunity for you to discover your own self, unravel who you are and build confidence in your abilities? Do you think looking at yourself for yourself and by yourself will help you understand this situation differently?"

Utkarsh looked at her, his expression softening slightly. "I hadn't thought of it that way. It's just hard to see the positive when I feel so abandoned."

Ms. Menon smiled gently. "It's absolutely challenging, and it's okay to feel overwhelmed. But it's also a chance for growth. How about we take a step back and reflect on some of the things you've managed on your own since Sheena left? Can you share some examples?"

Utkarsh hesitated, then slowly nodded. "Well, I did manage to settle into my new job. I've made some new friends, and I'm starting to enjoy the work. And I guess I've been handling living on my own better than I expected."

Ms. Menon's smile widened. "That's great, Utkarsh. These achievements show that you are capable and resilient, even if it doesn't always feel that way. How do you feel when you think about these successes?"

Utkarsh's expression brightened a little. "I feel... proud, I guess. It feels good to know I can handle things on my own, even if it's tough."

Ms. Menon nodded encouragingly. "Exactly. It's important to acknowledge these successes and build on them. It's also okay to feel sadness and bitterness; those emotions are part of the process. But by recognising your strengths, you can start to find a balance. You don't have to let go of the past entirely, but you can integrate these new experiences and strengths into your sense of self."

Utkarsh took a deep breath, a glimmer of hope in his eyes. "I think I understand. It's not about forgetting Sheena or what she meant to me, but about learning to stand on my own, finding my own path, and for both of us to find balance for each other in this new phase of life."

Ms. Menon smiled warmly. "That's right, Utkarsh. This journey is about embracing your independence and discovering your own identity, while still cherishing the bond you have with Sheena. It's a process, and it's okay to take it one step at a time."

Utkarsh nodded, feeling a newfound sense of determination. "Thank you, Ms. Menon. I think I'm ready to think about moving forward."

Ms. Menon's smile was reassuring. "You're doing great, Utkarsh. Remember, it's okay to feel a range of emotions, and it's okay to seek support when you need it. You're not alone in this journey."

In the course of the next few weeks, Utkarsh focused on making more changes in his life, gaining new experiences, and understanding himself more. He started to feel better about himself, though not fully himself just yet. He began to realize and accept the dependency that he had on Sheena and how a simple feeling of missing someone and letting go of her physically became such a difficult process for him.

As Utkarsh sat in the therapist's office again, it started to feel more familiar and comfortable.

Ms. Menon greeted him and said, "So, Utkarsh, how have you been since our last session?"

Utkarsh took a deep breath, collecting his thoughts. "It's been interesting and overwhelming at the same time. The city is so alive, and I've been learning so much in my new job and living away from family. But, I also miss home and Sheena. It's been a challenge to balance everything but it's not as bad as I thought."

Ms. Menon nodded. "I can imagine. It sounds like a significant transition. I'd like to know more about how this change has been for you. Is there anything you have learned about yourself since you left home?"

Utkarsh thought for a moment. "I've learned that I'm stronger and more independent than I thought, like you pointed out the last time. I've been able to settle into this new city, manage my job, share a living space, and meet new people. I've learnt that burnt is also a taste! I feel like I can handle a few things on my own. Earlier, I thought that I needed Sheena for everything, but it's been exciting to learn to stand on my own two feet"

"That's a wonderful realization, I'm glad to hear that you've been adjusting well and picking up new skills." Ms. Menon said. "You mentioned Sheena was there for you through everything before, but now that you're creating a new life for yourself, it seems to be working out better than you had imagined. Would you be comfortable talking about your relationship with Sheena and how it has changed?

"Hmm. I'm surprised that I'm saying this – but I think I feel differently about us. Because we grew up together and always had each other, I think I never really had to believe in myself enough to handle things on my own. Don't get me wrong – I loved her support and thrived with it, but now I'm realizing that not having her there for everything that happens in my life is actually helping me learn more about myself. I still do wish we were in the same city though; I miss having her around."

Ms. Menon: "Of course. It's only natural to miss each other's presence. But I'm glad you're learning so much about yourself now! I'd like to focus on that a bit more- seeing yourself beyond your relationship."

"Sure, in fact now that I think about it, I wonder if my behaviour may have felt a little suffocating for Sheena - as if she always had to consider my feelings before she could do anything for herself. I never wanted to be a burden on her like that."

Ms. Menon responded: "I can understand why you feel like you may have been a burden. It's also interesting that you're able to think from Sheena's perspective. However, her putting you first seems to have been a conscious choice on her end - to look out for you, as a way of showing you that you are a priority for her. Do you think it would help to share your reflection today with Sheena? It might be best to hear from her what she really felt like."

Utkarsh left the therapy session in a somber mood, carrying all these reflections with him. Later that evening, Utkarsh sat at his desk, the evening light casting a warm glow across his room. He took a deep breath and called Sheena on Facetime hoping they could have a conversation about all that had been on his mind since his counseling session. The phone rang twice before she picked up.

"Hey, Utkarsh," Sheena's voice came through, familiar and comforting. "How's everything?"

"Hey, Sheena. It's been good. I wanted to talk to you about something important," Utkarsh said, his voice steady yet hopeful.

"Of course, what's on your mind?" Sheena asked, her tone curious but gentle.

"I've been doing a lot of thinking lately," Utkarsh began. "About us, our relationship, and how we've both been feeling since we started living in different cities. I know it's been hard, and I've realized some things about myself and us."

Sheena listened intently, sensing the gravity of the conversation. "Go on," she encouraged.

"I've come to understand that I was too dependent on you, Sheena. I leaned on you for everything, and I never really gave you the space to pursue your own dreams without feeling guilty. I want to apologise for that," Utkarsh said, his voice filled with sincerity.

"Utkarsh, I appreciate you saying that," Sheena replied, her voice softening. "I never saw it as a burden, but sometimes I felt torn between supporting you and following my own path. I always wanted the best for both of us."

"I know you did, and I want that too," Utkarsh said. "That's why I think we need to find a better balance together, support each other's dreams while still being there for one another. I'd like more open communication about our individual needs and dreams. And I want us to build a relationship based on interdependence, not dependency."

Sheena nodded in agreement: "I think you're right. Being apart has made me realize how much I miss you and still value my independence, and I want to ensure we both have that space to grow individually. I want us to share our lives with each other without feeling the burden of disappointment. I truly hope we are able to communicate more openly about things in our lives, just like we used to."

"I agree," Utkarsh said, feeling a sense of relief and renewed hope. "I want us to build a relationship where we support each other but don't lose ourselves. We can be strong together without being overly reliant on one another."

"That sounds like a conscious task for both of us," Sheena said, her voice thoughtful. "I miss you, Utkarsh, but I've also been discovering a lot about myself here in New York. I think we can make this work if we both commit to understanding and respecting each other's journeys."

"Absolutely," Utkarsh said, "Let's promise to be honest about our feelings and support each other. We can make this long-distance relationship work if we both put in the effort."

"Deal," Sheena said, a smile in her voice. "I'm glad we had this conversation, Utkarsh. It means a lot to me."

"Me too, Sheena," Utkarsh said. "I believe in us, and I know we can build something even stronger than before."

They continued to talk; their conversation filled with new discoveries about each other. They were more prepared to embrace the newness in each other with understanding and mutual respect. As the evening turned to night, they both felt a deeper connection with each other, ready to face the challenges ahead with a clearer vision of their relationship's future.

Their journey was far from over, this conversation marked a significant step towards building a relationship grounded in both love and individual growth.

1. What does interdependence mean to me, and how is it different from dependency?

2. How do I feel when my needs are balanced in a relationship?

3. What needs do I need to fulfill for my loved ones?

4. How can I continue to grow both individually and within my relationships over time?

Overthinking

Pause

5

Overthinking

The Mind's Maze

> *Overthinking is like a rocking chair. It gives you something to do but gets you nowhere.*
>
> *– Jodi Picoult*

In the heart of a quiet suburb, where each house tells a story and the evenings are tranquil, Priya and Gaurav's home harbours a silent storm. The shadow of Gaurav's change of career from a stable job to his own start-up loomed heavily over the couple.

Priya grew up in a traditional household where stability and security were paramount. Her father worked a steady government job, and her mother managed the household with meticulous care. From a young age, Priya was taught that a stable job was the foundation of a secure life. This upbringing instilled in her a deep-seated belief that taking risks, especially financial ones, was irresponsible and reckless. When Priya graduated from college, she followed the path laid out for her, securing a stable job in a reputed company. This job became not just her career but a symbol of the stability she had always valued.

In contrast, Gaurav was raised in an environment that celebrated innovation and entrepreneurship. His parents, both risk takers and growth oriented, encouraged him to think outside the box and embrace challenges. Gaurav's childhood was filled with stories of startups, failures, and eventual successes. He grew up believing that taking calculated risks was essential for personal and professional growth. He had begun earning his own pocket money early in life with odd jobs even though his parents could afford things for him. After working in a corporate job for several years, Gaurav felt a growing desire to start his own business, driven by a passion for innovation and a belief in his ability to create something meaningful. The current environment, abuzz with unicorns emerging every other week and the government actively promoting entrepreneurship, further fueled his enthusiasm. Ideas were getting funded every day, and Gaurav saw this as the perfect time to take the leap and give his own ideas wings. The startup needed funding which has been secured by dipping into Gaurav's savings with the possibility of no profit for 12–24 months. While Gaurav had meticulously planned the finances, there were months when things didn't go as expected. It had been 14 months now, and Priya had begun to question this decision.

As she drove back from work, the drive sent her into an overdrive of countless scenarios, each filled with anxiety and fear. This habit of overthinking was now seeping into other areas of her life, affecting her work, social interactions, and even her health.

Have you found yourself in a situation similar to Priya's? When it felt like your mind had a mind of its own?

Recall that situation in your life. Did you feel like you were drowning in a sea of "what ifs", or did it bring you clarity? Is it healthy for you?

The space between Priya and Gaurav grew, filled with unspoken words and unresolved tensions. Priya's overthinking turned their conversations into minefields, where each word was carefully chosen, yet still felt inadequate. She could only visualize the things that had gone off plan and the things that would go off plan. She knew that this pattern of overthinking was a thief, stealing moments of peace and replacing them with endless cycles of worry.

The situation reached a new level when Priya was invited to speak at an international conference on education, a professional milestone. Gaurav, excited by her achievement, suggested he accompany her, envisioning it as a turning point for them both. The idea of extending the trip into a vacation, to celebrate, seemed like the perfect plan. However, Priya's excitement was quickly clouded by overthinking. The prospect of making decisions about the trip, from planning the itinerary to managing the dynamics of their relationship in an unfamiliar setting, to hanging out with her colleagues and Gaurav together, became another puzzle to solve, another outcome to predict and plan for.

Her overthinking mirrored her approach to decision-making in all areas of her life. Each potential joy was counterbalanced by a fear, each step forward shadowed by the possibility of a misstep. The vacation, meant to be a celebration and a step toward healing, turned into yet another battleground for her thoughts.

Just as Priya did, why do some of us go down this rabbit hole?

As many as 70% of adults find themselves entangled in the web of overthinking, a condition that fortunately for some of us, doesn't pervade every aspect of life but can significantly impact certain areas. We may overthink about the drinking habits of loved ones, the health of a child or key life decisions. This tendency to overanalyze is akin to possessing a peculiar skill: the ability to transform straightforward, potentially joyful situations into complex conundrums. It's as if we're perpetually solving a mental Rubik's Cube, endlessly twisting and turning our thoughts in search of resolution. Despite our best efforts to dissect and examine every angle, we often find ourselves emerging from these mental gymnastics with more confusion than clarity.

For some, overthinking serves as a misguided attempt at control. There's an underlying belief that by meticulously analyzing every possible detail, we can somehow improve our chances of controlling the outcome, ensuring that everything unfolds without a hitch. We chase the illusion of perfection, believing that if we can anticipate and plan for every conceivable scenario, we can avoid complications, maintain high standards, and prevent any potential problems.

Ironically, this trait can sometimes be rewarded, especially in professional settings. Our thoroughness and attention to detail might earn us accolades for being diligent and meticulous. Overthinking often masquerades as productivity or procrastination. In the depths of our analysis, we feel engaged, perhaps even indispensable, mistaking the endless cycle of speculation for meaningful work. This sense of utility feeds into the cycle, reinforcing the habit despite its detrimental effects. However, this praise comes at a steep price, as the constant mental strain of overthinking takes a toll on our well-being.

Have you ever mistaken overthinking for productivity? How can you identify the difference between productive reflection and unproductive rumination?

Signs you are an overthinker

1. **Sleeplessness**
2. **Second Guessing Decisions**
3. **Replay events**
4. **What if / Why Me?**
5. **Read between the lines**
6. **Inability to concentrate**

For Priya, overthinking felt like carrying an invisible weight on her shoulders, a burden that grew heavier with each passing thought. It was as if her mind was a maze with no exit, with the emergency exit keys in Gaurav's hands – "only if he takes a stable job!" The constant barrage of "what if-s" and worst-case scenarios drained her energy, leaving her exhausted and overwhelmed. She often found herself lost in thought, replaying conversations, second-guessing decisions, and imagining countless outcomes, most of which never came to pass. This mental overload not only affected her emotionally but also took a toll on her physical health, sleepless nights, headaches, and a perpetual sense of unease.

This constant state of mental turmoil not only distanced Priya from the joys of being in the present but also from her husband. Gaurav, too, felt the weight of her concerns, sensing the barrier they were creating. It's as though Priya was physically there with him, yet miles away, lost in a sea of thoughts from which she could not find her way back. Would it help for her to remember to have faith in Gaurav, in the fact that he has the best interest of the family in mind, just as much as she does?

Sometimes, we can find ourselves in situations where it's difficult to know when we have crossed the line from healthy analysis to overthinking.

There is a thin line between overthinking and reflection and one needs to be aware and catch themselves when crossing over. Catch yourself before you take that unnecessary spin on the merry-go-round of overthinking.

1. How does your overthinking affect your relationships with loved ones (like Priya and Gaurav)? Does it lead to misunderstandings or difficulty communicating openly?

2. Do you find, like the passage suggests, that overthinking sometimes stems from a good place, a desire for control or to avoid problems? How can you channel this positive intention into healthier thought patterns?

3. What are your personal triggers for overthinking? Are there certain situations or emotions that make you more prone to it?

4. When you feel yourself going down the overthinking rabbit hole, what strategies could you employ to interrupt the pattern?

5. How can you strike a balance between healthy reflection and unhealthy overthinking?

Pause

Find Clarity in Stillness

> "*A pause gives you breathing space so listen to the whispers of the real you waiting to happen.*"
>
> *– Tara Estacaan*

Priya's struggle with overthinking isn't just about fearing the unknown; it's about an intense longing to steer their life towards a semblance of perfection—a perfection that, in her eyes, could shield them from unpredictability. Yet, this quest for control is a mirage, an elusive goal that slips further away the harder she tries to grasp it.

The irony of Priya's situation is that in her attempt to create a flawless life, she often overlooks the beauty in the imperfections—the missteps and miscommunications that, while challenging, have strengthened their bond over time. The laughter that bubbles up after a misunderstanding, the warmth of a reconciliatory hug, and the comfort of shared silence after a stormy argument; these are the moments that truly define their journey together.

Her preoccupation with managing the future means that the present often passes by unnoticed. The quiet evenings spent side by side, the spontaneous outings that break the monotony of routine, and the joy of impromptu dance sessions in their living room—these instances of unguarded happiness are overshadowed by the looming cloud of her worries.

In this dance of love and worry, Priya and Gaurav find themselves at a crossroads, where the path to harmony is clouded by the fog of overthinking. It's a journey that requires not just the courage to face the unknown but the wisdom to appreciate the beauty of the now—to find joy in the simple pleasures of their life together, unmarred by the specter of 'what ifs'. Simple pauses can help her reconnect with the now. But this is easier said than done, and we all know that! Here are some ways she can create small pauses in her life.

One afternoon in the office Priya was mindlessly scrolling short videos when she came across a parable.

Once, in a bustling village, there was a wise old farmer known for his calm demeanor and thoughtful actions. One day, his horse ran away. The villagers came to console him, saying, "What bad luck!" The farmer simply replied, "Maybe."

A week later, the horse returned with a group of wild horses. The villagers exclaimed, "What good fortune!" Again, the farmer said, "Maybe."

Soon after, the farmer's son tried to ride one of the wild horses, but he was thrown off and broke his leg. The villagers came to express their sympathy, saying, "What a tragedy!" The farmer responded, "Maybe."

A few weeks later, the army came to the village to recruit young men for war. Seeing the farmer's son with a broken leg, they left him behind. The villagers said, "What a blessing!" The farmer again replied, "Maybe."

The farmer's ability to pause and refrain from immediate judgment allowed him to stay calm and see the bigger picture. By not rushing to label events as good or bad, he maintained a balanced perspective, demonstrating the power and wisdom of taking a pause before reacting.

She reflected a bit and started a conversation with her colleague over lunch and realized that the concept of 'pause' is about intentionally taking a momentary break from the constant flow of thoughts and actions to gain clarity, reset emotions, and make more mindful decisions. Pauses help interrupt the cycle of overthinking and allows for a more balanced and thoughtful response to situations. It is essential because it prevents us from being overwhelmed by our thoughts, reduces stress, and enhances our ability to focus on the present moment, thus improving our overall mental well-being.

Pausing is crucial as it creates a mental space where we

can step back from our immediate reactions and reflect on our thoughts and feelings. This break can prevent hasty decisions driven by stress or anxiety, allowing us to approach problems with a clearer mind and a more balanced perspective. By incorporating pauses into our daily routine, we can better manage stress, improve our emotional regulation, and foster a greater sense of calm and control in our lives.

Pause & Sigh

Yes, go ahead and just take a sigh and feel the difference that a bit of a pause makes! Deep breathing activates the parasympathetic nervous system, which helps reduce stress levels. A study published in Frontiers in Psychology (2017) found that controlled breathing can decrease stress, increase alertness, and boost one's emotional state. This simple act signals the brain to calm down and return to the present moment.

Try the Five Senses Grounding Exercise which helps bring your focus back to the present moment by engaging your senses. Start by noticing five things you can see, four things you can touch, three things you can hear, two things you can smell, and one thing you can taste. This simple yet effective technique can calm your mind, reduce anxiety, and interrupt the cycle of overthinking by anchoring you in the here and now.

Ⓘ Pause & Talk to the Ducks

Ducks or birds or dogs or cats, any loving animal will do! Just picking your choice and interacting with nature, even just spending time in a park, can significantly improve mental health. Research in the Journal of Environmental Psychology (2010) highlights that natural environments promote emotional well-being and reduce feelings of social isolation. Speaking your worries out loud, even to animals, can help you from a new perspective, often revealing solutions or alleviating the burden.

Ⓘ Pause for Decision-Making

Setting a timer for decision-making is rooted in the idea of 'analysis paralysis', where overanalyzing leads to decision fatigue. A study in the Journal of Personality and Social Psychology found that limiting the time for making decisions can increase satisfaction and reduce the stress associated with making the 'perfect' choice. As they say, "bad decisions make great stories!"

Ⓘ Pause & Share

Sharing thoughts and feelings with others can significantly reduce stress and improve mental health. A vast body of research underscores the importance of social support in emotional regulation and problem-solving. When we articulate our thoughts, we often gain new insights and perspectives, making our worries more manageable.

Pause with Physical Activity

Engaging in physical activity is not just beneficial for physical health but is also a potent antidote to overthinking. Exercise releases endorphins, known as 'feel-good' hormones, which act as natural stress relievers. According to the American Journal of Psychiatry (2018), regular physical activity is associated with improved mental health.

Pause to Notice the Small Things

Acknowledging a small win, a small moment with someone (even a stranger sometimes) or paying attention to the small details of our surroundings, can significantly promote well-being. This practice of awareness brings us back to the present, helping to break the cycle of rumination and worry.

Pause & Laugh

Laughter triggers the release of endorphins, promoting an overall sense of well-being. Research indicates that laughter can reduce stress, increase pain tolerance, and improve immune function. From inane Instagram reels to YouTube videos of stand-up comics, to PJs with friends, try them for a chuckle. It's a powerful tool for bringing us back to the present and lifting the weight of overthinking.

⏸ Pause & Have Faith

Take a moment to trust in the process, your abilities, and the support of those around you and the universe. It involves letting go of the need to control every outcome and believing that things will work out, even if not as planned. Having faith can reduce the stress and anxiety associated with overthinking, providing a sense of peace and perspective. Trusting in yourself, your loved ones, and the universe can create mental space to focus on the present, appreciate the journey, and foster resilience in the face of uncertainty.

⏸ Tackle One Thing at a Time

Focusing on one task at a time can reduce feelings of overwhelm and increase efficiency. Multitasking has been shown to increase cortisol levels, the stress hormone, leading to higher anxiety. Breaking tasks down and focusing on them individually helps manage stress and improves productivity.

⏸ Book end your day with gratitude

Gratitude has been extensively studied for its positive effects on mental health. Keeping a gratitude journal or simply taking time to reflect on things you're thankful for can shift focus from overthinking to appreciation. Bookend your day by starting and ending your day with a gratitude note on your phone. Three things you are grateful for today. Research in the Journal of Personality and Social Psychology demonstrates that gratitude is strongly associated with greater happiness, helping people feel more positive emotions, relish good experiences, and build strong relationships.

A pause is a conscious decision to step back from immediate emotional reactions, allowing space for clarity and reflection. It's about taking a breath, creating distance from the urgency of the moment, and giving yourself permission to process your thoughts and feelings in a measured way. Unlike avoidance, pausing doesn't mean ignoring the issue at hand; it's about postponing the discussion or decision until you are in a better state of mind to address it effectively.

In the TV series *How I Met Your Mother,* Lily and Marshall exemplify the power of pause in their relationship. When tensions rise during a disagreement, they agree to put a temporary halt to the argument. This isn't about sweeping problems under the rug, but rather acknowledging that sometimes, the heat of the moment isn't the best time to resolve issues. By putting a pin in it and returning to the conversation when they're ready, they give themselves the space to think more clearly and communicate more effectively.

1. What would Pause look like for you?

2. Think about the times you struggle with overthinking. What "pause" techniques could you experiment with in those situations?

3. How can you integrate pausing into your daily routine? Can you identify specific times of day or triggers that would be good reminders to pause?

4. When was the last time you truly appreciated a simple moment in the present? How can you cultivate a greater awareness of the little joys in your life?

Anxiety

Recognition

6

Anxiety

More Than Just Worry

> “*Anxiety's like a rocking chair. It gives you something to do, but it doesn't get you very far.*”
>
> *– Jodi Picoult*

Sushmita has just begun working in a large MNC. At 45, Sushmita had dedicated years to personal growth and career ambitions, while her social life, particularly her dating life, had taken a backseat. She had started a new job and began carpooling with a colleague named Laila, a single mother eight years her senior. Their drives to and from work were filled with lively banter and laughter about everything under the sun. Laila was warm, humorous, and genuinely caring. One day, with the casualness of suggesting a new brand of tea, Laila proposed, “Why don't you try a dating app?”

Sushmita was apprehensive. She had a million rebuttals about the kind of people she might meet, the safety of online dating, and the potential pitfalls. Yet, after months of Laila's gentle encouragement, Sushmita took the plunge and signed up, albeit with a lingering sense of skepticism.

Connecting with someone on the app who shared her interests and worldview was refreshing. Soon enough, they set a time to meet in person. However, as the date drew closer, the joy she initially felt began to warp into a knot of anxiety. Dates were organic in her world—you met people in college and at parties (which was a decade ago for her), and she realized the world had moved on. What seemed exciting at first now felt daunting. Every decision, from choosing an outfit to selecting the venue, felt loaded with implications. Her mind raced with questions. What should she wear? Would a coffee shop setting strike the right balance between casual and thoughtful? What if they found themselves mired in awkward silence?

Caught in a whirlwind of overthinking, Sushmita agonised over outfit choices, discarding each option for being too formal, too casual, or too much of an attempt to impress. Sleep eluded her as she imagined every possible scenario, each under the magnifying glass of her insecurities. Her self-esteem, never particularly strong, was being battered by a storm of doubt.

On the morning of the first date, the physical symptoms of her anxiety were undeniable. Her stomach was in knots, her hands trembled as she tried to steady them, and a persistent headache served as a painful reminder of the night's restless thoughts. She was on the verge of canceling, overwhelmed by the fear of rejection, the dread of disappointment, and the vulnerability of opening up to a stranger, only to be found wanting. But then, she courageously took the chance and made her way to the meeting.

Laila encouraged her to meet more than one person and Sushmita managed to go on three different dates over the next few months, each with its own flavour.

Her first date was with Arjun, a literature professor. They connected over their love for books and had deep conversations about their favorite authors. However, as the date progressed, Sushmita became guarded, her energy changing as she adopted a rigid stance. Her mind began scanning for flaws, seeking to match them with her ideas and opinions about herself and relationships. She fixated on minor details—his slightly outdated fashion sense and the way he twirled his hair when thinking—and concluded they were incompatible.

Her second date was with Vikram, an avid traveler and photographer. He regaled her with stories of his adventures, sparking an initial excitement in Sushmita. Yet, the moment he suggested planning a trip together,

her anxiety took over. She became fidgety, and her mind raced with fears of stepping out of her comfort zone. Overwhelmed, she withdrew, citing her busy schedule.

Her third date was with Neeraj, a compassionate and patient listener. They had an immediate connection, sharing similar values and dreams. Despite feeling a genuine bond, Sushmita's familiar anxiety crept in, whispering that she didn't deserve someone as kind as Neeraj. Her mind scanned for flaws, convincing her that her negative beliefs were true. She distanced herself, running away from what could have been a meaningful relationship.

Sushmita realized she was caught in a cycle, finding faults in each person to protect herself from the vulnerability of connection. Her anxiety latched onto her insecurities, convincing her that this was how things had to function, that she was being responsible by scrutinizing every detail. Yet, she never got a break from her relentless thoughts.

The vicious cycle of anxiety begins with heightened vigilance and an incessant search for potential threats, accompanied by irrational thoughts about how things could go wrong. This fear of losing control often drives a desire to escape or avoid the triggering situation. While avoidance

may offer temporary relief, it can lead to increased anxiety and poor coping mechanisms in the long term. Over time, reliance on safety behaviours, such as avoiding social situations or seeking constant reassurance, becomes more prevalent. Although these behaviours are meant to protect, they often reinforce the anxiety, preventing individuals from effectively confronting and managing their fears. Breaking this cycle requires recognising and challenging these behaviours, gradually exposing oneself to feared situations, and developing healthier coping strategies to foster resilience and regain control.

We've all been there—hopefully on exciting first dates, but also having flirted with anxiety at some point. It is one of our most primal emotions, as inherent to our being as the very air we breathe at birth. Understanding anxiety means seeing the whole range of it—from a brief, mild worry to overwhelming feelings that mess up your day. Knowing when anxiety is just passing by and when it's a sign of something more serious is important. The strength and how often these feelings happen can tell you if you need help or not.

Anxiety, at its core, is a natural response designed to protect us from danger, like an internal alarm system that prepares us to face challenges. Its intentions are good, aiming to keep us safe by heightening our awareness and readiness. However, when anxiety becomes excessive, it transforms from a protective mechanism into a formidable barrier. Instead of safeguarding us, it holds us back, limiting our engagement with the world and preventing us from embracing new experiences. This overwhelming anxiety can make us feel boxed in, as if confined within invisible walls that isolate us from the richness of life. It's as if the protective instinct has overstepped its bounds, restricting our freedom and clouding our perspective.

What is the role anxiety plays in your life? Do you feel like it takes over your life or is it under your control?

In a way, anxiety can motivate us to prepare and take action. This anxiety is healthy and appropriate; it's the feeling we experience before an exam, an important meeting, or a big decision. This anxiety gets us out of bed and gets us to do things that move us forward. Anxiety helps us to be cautious, anticipate obstacles, and encourages us to stay organized and on track. It acts as a monitor, alerting us to potential threats or dangers, often referred to as a gut feeling, guiding us to navigate life's challenges with heightened awareness and readiness.

The real challenge is telling the difference between the kind of anxiety that motivates us and the kind that's too much to handle, like the nervousness before an exam versus a constant fear that affects how you see life. The line can blur quickly for some of us.

If you know someone who is worried almost all the time about many things, even when there might not be a big reason to worry, it is possible that they are dealing with anxiety. For others, social situations and the fear of feeling judged or embarrassed sets off anxiety. And for others , sudden and intense episodes of fear can come out of nowhere, which could lead to a state of panic. You may even know someone who constantly avoids specific things like heights, spiders, or the sight of blood, because it makes them feel intense fear.

It's crucial to notice when you are anxious and how it's affecting you. Figuring out when it's pushing you to do better and when it's holding you back is key. Anxiety isn't just something you feel in your mind; it can affect your body too, making your heart race, your hands sweat, or your stomach turn. But there comes a point when anxiety stops helping and starts getting in the way of living well. You know you need support when the anxiety seems to be too excessive – when it becomes overwhelming with all possible negativity and dreadful thoughts, and you feel uncomfortable to the point where nothing seems to help, and you can't seem to understand it, no matter what you do.

And then there is high-functioning anxiety. It isn't an official diagnosis, but it's a term often used to describe people who manage to keep up with their daily responsibilities, perform well at work or school, and appear to be functioning well in their social lives, despite struggling with anxiety internally in silence. These are overachievers or perfectionists, constantly pushing themselves, often out of fear of failure or letting others down. On the surface, they seem to have everything under control, but underneath, they might be dealing with constant worry, fear, restlessness, and other anxiety symptoms. They may also have trouble relaxing or constantly feel overwhelmed, though they're good at hiding these feelings from others. High-functioning anxiety can be exhausting and stressful, and people dealing with it might find it hard to ask for help or take time for self-care, fearing it could disrupt their ability to cope or maintain their high standards.

The Diathesis-Stress Model explains how anxiety develops through a mix of inherited traits and life experiences. If you have a family history of anxiety or tend to think negatively, you're more likely to develop anxiety when faced with stress. Stress generators like traumatic events or feeling isolated can trigger anxiety. The more vulnerable you are, the less stress you need to trigger anxiety, while those with lower vulnerability need more stress. Having good support and strong coping skills can help protect you from developing anxiety.

Knowing what sets off your anxiety and asking for help when you need it are important steps in dealing with these tough feelings. At its core, anxiety is often about fear, making us imagine the worst and keeping us stuck in a cycle of worry.

In the end, anxiety is a normal part of being human, but it needs to be balanced. We have to recognise when it's driving us forward and when we need to take a step back and take care of ourselves, especially when we worry too much about the little things.

1. Identify situations that tend to trigger your anxiety, how do you typically respond to them?

2. What are some signs that indicate that you are anxious? (Eg: nail biting, heart racing, palm sweating etc)

3. Can you reflect on a time when anxiety made you feel boxed in and held you back?

4. Have you found yourself avoiding situations or tasks due to anxiety? What would it look like if you were to face these situations?

Recognition

Finding Your Calm

> ***Control is merely an illusion we construct to cope with the chaos that is reality.***
>
> ***– Fred Bubbers***

After a particularly sleepless night, Sushmita had an epiphany. Her anxiety, which had been posing as a shield, was actually a barrier to the life she wanted. What she really wanted was to be more open, feel more connected to people, and form meaningful relationships in her life. She realized she was coming in her own way, but didn't quite understand how or what to do about it. Determined to break free, she decided to seek professional help and see a therapist.

The journey to finding the right therapist was daunting. Sushmita was hesitant, worried about opening up to a stranger and whether she would be able to find someone who truly understood her unique challenges. She researched extensively, reading reviews and seeking recommendations, wanting to ensure she found someone who resonated with her needs and personality.

After a few trial sessions with different therapists, Sushmita finally connected with Dr. Neha, whose calm demeanor and empathetic listening made her feel at ease.

In her first therapy session with Dr. Neha, Sushmita began to unpack her recent dating experiences. Dr. Neha listened intently, nodding with understanding as Sushmita recounted the details of each encounter, focusing on the flaws she had found in her dates. Dr. Neha seemed to have a real understanding of what was worrying Sushmita. Her apprehension about opening up to a stranger faded quickly as she found all her feelings spilling out of her, almost automatically. As Sushmita spoke, Dr. Neha gently guided the conversation deeper, seeking to explore the underlying reasons for Sushmita's actions.

"Sushmita, I'm curious," Dr. Neha began, her voice soft yet probing, "what do you feel when you start finding these flaws in people? What goes through your mind?"

Sushmita raised her eyebrows and exclaimed "I feel like I'm crazy! Like I'm scrutinizing everything much more than others do, and I just can't understand why I do that."

"Hmm", Dr. Neha looked thoughtful, "All our behaviour usually tends to have some payoff. Something that has worked for us in the past, maybe, that we feel would help now? It may not be entirely helpful, but it usually tends to have a little bit of good in it. Do you think there might be something good, something helpful that comes out of finding these flaws in people? Some purpose this fulfills?"

Many of our behaviors are designed to shield us from disappointment, hurt, and psychological discomfort that we might encounter in the future. Our protective brain swiftly deploys its tools to safeguard and defend against situations that may seem beyond our control. These tools are known as defense mechanisms—strategies we learn and develop as we navigate through life. While these mechanisms once helped us cope effectively, they may not always be as beneficial in every situation. Over time, what once served as a protective barrier can sometimes become a hindrance, preventing us from fully engaging with the present and adapting to new challenges. Recognising and understanding these mechanisms can help us choose more adaptive and constructive ways to handle life's complexities.

Sushmita paused, her brow furrowing in thought. "I suppose knowing their flaws prepares me for the worst. If I'm aware of them beforehand, I won't be caught off guard when they disappoint me. It makes me feel more in control, like I'm shielding myself from potential hurt. My anxiety always has me thinking of the worst-case scenarios, so I'm never surprised because my mind has already played them out for me."

Dr. Neha nodded thoughtfully and asked, "That's an interesting way to look at your anxiety. What do you think you're truly trying to protect yourself from?" encouraging Sushmita to delve deeper.

The question lingered in the air. Sushmita was silent for a moment, the wheels turning in her head. She had always viewed her critical eye as a form of self-protection, yet she had never considered what she was protecting herself from.

Dr. Neha saw the confusion and hesitation in Sushmita's expression and decided to delve deeper into her beliefs. "Often, we protect ourselves because we carry beliefs about our worth or what we deserve. Do any thoughts come to mind about why you might feel the need to push people away?"

Sushmita sighed, a mix of resignation and revelation washing over her. "Maybe... maybe I'm scared they won't really like me if they get to know me. They'll find out how weird I can be, how much I worry, how I'm not all that funny or cool. All the bad things about me, basically. That I'm just not good enough to be with. ."

Dr. Neha nodded, her expression compassionate. "That sounds like a very heavy belief to carry with you. It's understandable that it would affect how you interact with others. Do you feel this belief may be playing a role in how you approach relationships?"

"Yes, I think it does," Sushmita admitted, her voice softening. "I don't know if I'll ever find anyone who's right for me. I have so much anxiety about relationships, about being vulnerable. It's terrifying to think about opening up to someone."

Dr. Neha smiled gently, her gaze supportive. "Thank you for sharing that, Sushmita. It's a big step to recognise these feelings. Let's explore these fears and see how we can work through them together."

As the session continued, Dr. Neha helped Sushmita to understand that her habit of finding flaws in others was a defense mechanism that was stemming from the anxieties she held close, it was a way to avoid the vulnerability that comes with true intimacy.

The genesis of anxiety lies in fear, which is the function of the need to control. Many analogies come to my mind when I think of anxiety. Imagine sitting in a room and a cat walks in. Would you be scared? Maybe not, but at the same time, if a bigger cat like a leopard or tiger is looking outside our room, a fear would be much greater. The psychological reason for this is that we know that we can control a situation with a cat, however, bigger cats may be stronger and overpowering, making the brain feel no control over the situation. However if you are a trained vet or caretaker for bigger cats, your skills are developed to manage the situation. Another analogy is to imagine on the top of a ten story building and you decide to walk on the edge of it. What would you feel? Great anxiety, panic and fear. However, if you decide to learn gymnastics and then go back on the top of the same, 10 story building, will the panic, be the same? Probably not. Nothing changed. The height of the building is still the same. If we fall, the consequences will still be the same. However, by learning gymnastics, our brain feels that it has the skills to navigate and manage one's own self in the situation.

Sushmita took this reflection back with her, and her behaviour started to make a little more sense. The farther back she went in her memories of her life, she could find more and more traces of this belief and similar behavior. In a way it was a daunting reflection, but she felt relieved to know herself a little bit better.

In the next session, Dr. Neha encouraged Sushmita to look within her. After multiple conversations about her anxiety, anxiety was identified as a character in her inner world, one that emerges as an unwelcome visitor, an ever-present character in Sushmita's mind. This character, although not invited, becomes a constant companion, never leaving and persistently chattering away. It causes Sushmita to second-guess every little thing she does, making her feel as though she's under perpetual scrutiny. Anxiety's voice is critical and judgmental, never allowing for peace or quiet. It seems to latch onto one concern, and as soon as that issue is resolved, it finds another problem to highlight. Living with this internal critic is exhausting. Anxiety's constant scrutiny makes it hard for Sushmita to open up to men who are interested in her, pushing away the chance of finding a potential life partner.

"Let's try a different approach today," Dr. Neha suggested, her voice calm and inviting. "We'll explore the part of you that holds your anxiety. Think of it as getting to know a part of yourself better."

Sushmita nodded, a mix of curiosity and apprehension in her eyes.

"Where in your body do you feel this anxious part?" Dr. Neha started, guiding Sushmita to become aware of it in her body.

"It's in my chest," Sushmita replied, her hand moving to her heart. "It feels tight, like it's hard to breathe."

"Focus on that tightness," Dr. Neha directed. "What images or words come to mind when you think about this part?"

Sushmita closed her eyes, breathing deeply. "It's like a tangled ball of wires. It's chaotic and noisy."

Dr. Neha nodded, writing down notes. "How old do you think this part is? What emotions are emerging as you focus on it?"

"It feels young... scared. It's like it's about my age when I first felt attracted to a boy in school. I was really anxious, we were made to believe that this was the time to focus on studies and nothing else."

"How do you feel towards this part right now while talking about it?" Dr. Neha continued, looking intently at Sushmita.

"I'm frustrated with it," Sushmita admitted. "It holds me back. Because it was ingrained in me that I shouldn't focus on other things during school, I feel like I missed out on being with someone who liked me. I spent my entire life focusing on everything but love and look where it's gotten me. I'm alone and terrified about opening up to people. "

"Let's try to understand this part of you," Dr. Neha suggested softly. "What do you think this part would like you to know? What is its purpose?"

Sushmita took a moment to reflect, the atmosphere in the room heavy with her introspection. "I think it wants to protect me," she finally said, her voice quivering slightly with newfound understanding. "It's scared that if I open up, I'll be vulnerable, and that vulnerability will lead to hurt. So, it keeps me on high alert, always looking for signs of rejection or disappointment."

Dr. Neha nodded, encouraging her to go deeper. "What is this part afraid would happen if it stopped doing its job? If it stopped protecting you in this way?"

Sushmita's eyes widened as she considered the question. "I suppose... it fears that I'll be hurt, really hurt, and that I won't be able to handle it. It's like this part thinks I'm still that young girl, too fragile to face the world's realities without its protection."

Dr. Neha gently urged her forward. "It seems like this part has been carrying a heavy burden for a long time. Imagine asking it if it's ready to relax a little, to trust that you have grown and learned how to handle disappointments and setbacks in healthier ways. How does that feel?"

Sushmita paused, taking a deep breath as she engaged with this idea. "It feels... liberating, yet scary. But maybe it's time to let this part know I'm not that vulnerable girl anymore. I'm stronger now, and maybe it's okay for us to start letting go of that constant vigilance."

Dr. Neha smiled, acknowledging the progress. "That's a powerful realisation, Sushmita. This is how we start to negotiate with our parts, by recognising their intentions and gently guiding them towards new roles as we grow. Let's explore how we can support this part in trusting your current strengths and resilience."

What does your anxiety look like?

Start by identifying the part of you that holds anxiety.

Where in your body do you feel this anxious part?

What thoughts, words, or images does it bring to mind? Focus on this part in your body and notice what emerges.

Explore this part by considering how old it might be, the emotions it evokes, and what else you notice about it.

> **Then, move to understanding your feelings towards this part—do you feel anger, fear, compassion?**
>
> **What does this part want you to know about its role and purpose in your life? What might happen if it stopped doing what it's doing?**
>
> **Reflecting on these questions will help you communicate with this part, understand its fears and motivations, and begin to foster a more harmonious internal environment where every part can be acknowledged and integrated into your being.**

In the later sessions, Dr. Neha introduced Sushmita to Acceptance and Commitment Therapy (ACT), a therapeutic approach designed to enhance psychological flexibility. She explained that ACT encourages individuals to live in the present moment, accept their thoughts and feelings without judgment, and align their actions with their core values. This approach struck a chord with Sushmita, who realized that her anxiety was deeply intertwined with a need for control and fear of the unknown.

Sushmita shared that she felt anxious whenever she received a message from someone she was dating. Dr. Neha asked her to describe what happened when she received these messages. Sushmita explained, "I notice my heart races and I start overthinking every word in the message. I worry if I've said something wrong or if they're losing interest."

Dr. Neha guided Sushmita to pinpoint the specific elements of these interactions that triggered her anxiety. "What is it about receiving these messages that makes you feel this way?" Sushmita reflected and said, "I think it's because I feel like I need to respond perfectly. If I don't, I fear they might think less of me or that I'm not good enough." Dr. Neha helped Sushmita connect this reaction to her broader pattern of needing reassurance and fearing rejection. "So, receiving messages triggers your anxiety because you feel pressure to respond in a way that will ensure their approval."

Sushmita agreed, recognising that her anxiety was triggered by the fear of making a mistake in her responses and the need for validation. This realization allowed her to start practicing mindfulness techniques to manage her reactions when she received messages, helping her respond more calmly and with less anxiety.

Through their sessions, Sushmita began to learn how to identify her triggers and practice mindfulness.

This practice enabled her to observe her thoughts without becoming overwhelmed. Through mindfulness exercises, she developed the ability to sit with her emotions and thoughts rather than being controlled by them. This shift allowed her to confront her negative beliefs and replace them with more compassionate and realistic perspectives.

Sushmita began to actively incorporate these insights into her dating life. She created a go-to list of cafes and restaurants where she felt comfortable and enjoyed spending time. When planning dates, she would suggest one of these favorite spots and then let her date choose the final venue. This approach helped her feel more at ease, as she was already familiar with the environment. She also embraced the idea of trying new places based on her date's suggestions, which made each outing feel like an adventure rather than a high-stakes event.

To ease the pressure of conversations, Sushmita started initiating discussions with lighthearted anecdotes or interesting tidbits she had picked up from social media. This approach allowed her to shift focus away from the dreaded interview-style conversations and instead engage in meaningful, enjoyable exchanges. By doing so, she approached each date with the intention of simply enjoying the moment, rather than obsessing over the outcome.

Sushmita found that her anxiety around choosing what to wear for dates still persisted, but she managed it by understanding what she felt most comfortable in. She spent some time reflecting on the fact that how she is perceived by another person may be out of her control, but what is in her control is making sure she is most comfortable and relaxed in what she is wearing. She gradually learned to value her own feelings about her style rather than relying on validation from others.

What this journey taught Sushmita was that the key to managing her anxiety lay not in exerting control over every aspect of her life but in fostering a sense of inner control. This inner control was not about meticulous planning or avoiding uncertainty, but about embracing mindfulness, making proactive decisions, and remaining flexible.

By acknowledging her need for control and learning to respond to life's uncertainties with a balanced approach, Sushmita shifted from feeling powerless to experiencing a sense of manageability. She realized that true control was less about dominating her environment and more about guiding her responses and actions in line with what truly mattered to her.

Her new goal became to relax and enjoy her dates, focusing on the potential for connection rather than stressing about the outcome. This shift in mindset allowed her to be more present and engaged during interactions, fostering a more genuine connection with others.

Embracing psychological flexibility, as guided by her therapy, helped Sushmita live more fully in the present moment. She learned to be kinder to herself, accepted her thoughts and feelings without judgment, and made choices that aligned with her values, even during challenging times. This new approach empowered her to face the uncertainties of dating with a renewed sense of confidence, understanding that true control lay in her ability to adapt and respond with grace and resilience.

1. How do you perceive your anxiety? Do you see it as a protector, a hindrance, or something else entirely?

2. In what areas do you feel the need for control the most? How does this need impact your actions and decisions?

3. What are some ways in which anxiety has helped you in the past? What might it be trying to protect you from now?

4. What could be the underlying fear or belief that fuels your anxiety?

Low Self-Esteem

Assurance

7

Low Self-Esteem

A Cage Built from Within

> *Low self-esteem is like driving through life with your hand-brake on.*
>
> – *Maxwell Maltz*

In the cozy corner of the office canteen, over steaming cups of evening chai, sat a group of friends. To anyone peeping in, this bunch seemed to have it all—fancy degrees, jobs that made others go 'wow', and homes straight out of a magazine. But if you leaned in a little closer, you'd hear a different story, one not so shiny.

Mia's job was all about making social media look fun and effortless, but every time she looked in the mirror, she felt tangled in a mess of self-doubt. Her life revolved around capturing the perfect picture, as impression management was crucial in her line of work. Yet, every time she logged onto social media, it felt like the whole world was at a grand party where she didn't quite belong. Her natural, untouched selfies never seemed to match the effortlessly perfect images others posted online. Editing her pictures with a bit of digital makeup became a habit, feeding the feeling that she wasn't as perfect as everyone else appeared to be. Beneath her curated feed, Mia struggled with feelings of inadequacy, often wondering if her real self would ever be enough.

Then there was Aradhana, the meticulous quality checker, who felt overshadowed by her brother—the family star. At home, it was always about him, leaving her in the dust and making her wonder if her own victories were ever big enough to get noticed. This feeling tagged along to her work, making her second-guess her every idea. She often sat silently in meetings, her voice drowned out by the echoes of her childhood, afraid that her contributions wouldn't measure up. Aradhana carried the weight of unspoken expectations, feeling as though she was constantly in a race she could never win. "Delulu is the new solulu," she'd mutter sarcastically when asked about her achievements, masking the sting of comparison with humor.

Aarav, the guy who could fix anything in operations, had a different story. His parents watched over him so closely growing up that he hardly had to make any big decisions on his own. Fast forward to now, and deciding on what sandwich to order can feel like a high-stakes game. This habit of hesitating has stuck around, making every choice at work a mountain to climb. Aarav felt trapped in a cycle of indecision, worried that each choice might lead to disaster. He often wished for the courage to trust his instincts but found himself paralysed by the fear of making a wrong move.

Samantha, the wordsmith, could write her way out of any problem but put her in a meeting, and suddenly, it was as if she'd lost her voice. Behind her screen, she was a wizard, but ask her to share her ideas out loud, and she clammed up, worried they might not be good enough. She was conscious of how people would judge her, especially when she was in large groups. Each meeting was a battle between her creative mind and her silenced voice, leaving her frustrated and defeated. Samantha longed to share her thoughts and be heard, but her fear of judgment kept her ideas locked away. She would much rather send an email than speak up in a meeting.

Leading this pack was Sidharth, the sales wizard, always smashing targets. But his drive wasn't just about loving a win; it was more about fearing a loss. Deep down, he worried that one slip-up might reveal he wasn't all he was cracked up to be, making each success just a way to keep those doubts at bay. He chased achievements to fill the void of self-doubt, afraid of being exposed as an imposter. Sidharth's outward confidence masked an inner turmoil, a constant fight to maintain the image of success he felt he needed to uphold.

Sitting around that table, you'd see a group that looked like they had the world at their feet. But inside, each of them was dealing with their own little whirlwind, wondering if they were enough, doubting their every move, and sometimes feeling a bit lost in the shuffle.

Low self-esteem is different from a sense of not feeling like you are good enough at something 'yet'. While the latter can motivate you to improve your abilities, low self-esteem is a belief that pervades across situations. It can also be self-perpetuating- a notion about low worth leading to behaviors that confirm those beliefs.

A sense of low self-esteem can sometimes start as early as during our childhood. As we grow and move about in our lives, the constant negative self-talk builds a narrative that stops us from progressing.

Our early childhood and adolescent experiences form our core beliefs which are strong, long-term beliefs that shape the way we understand how the world works and who we are.

The chatter in our head can get so loud that while the world sees Mia, Aradhana, Aarav, Samantha and Sidharth for their achievements, they don't find the courage to open the next door that takes them to better opportunities. The unhelpful assumptions leading to automatic negative thoughts, or in more psychological terms, cognitive distortions, create biased and distorted ways in which we see ourselves, our life, and our day-to-day situations. While these are a part of all human experiences, the unhelpful way of thinking and viewing ourselves takes a hit on our overall mental health.

Can you think of an area in your life where you feel that nagging sense of low self-esteem? Do you think that this belief is limiting to your life in any manner?

One evening, as the sun dipped below the horizon, Mia broke the silence, "Do you guys ever feel like you're just faking it?" Her confession opened a floodgate of shared insecurities and unspoken fears.

"Every decision feels like I'm choosing between saving the world or letting it burn," Aarav joked, attempting to lighten the mood. "Seriously, I overthink everything. Even choosing a sandwich feels like a big deal."

Mia laughed, "I get that. I know my Instagram profile looks all prim and proper, but in real life, I'm just trying to survive with everything happening all at once. It's hard to keep everything looking perfect! I wish I could be unfiltered—both literally and figuratively!"

"Tell me about it," Samantha chimed in. "I can write up a storm behind my screen, but put me in a meeting, and I'm suddenly mute. It's like I can't form a coherent thought, much less share my opinions and ideas. I don't know why, but it's so nerve-wracking putting myself out there.."

Aradhana nodded. "I know what you mean. I don't even live with my family anymore, but somehow in my head I'm always stuck in my brother's shadow - like I was throughout my childhood. Strangely, it doesn't leave me even now. It's exhausting!

"Guys, fake it till you make it, right?" Sidharth chimed in, trying to sound confident. "That's just how the world works. We're all just trying to keep it together."

"Yeah, but we all know it's easier said than done," Aarav replied. "Sometimes, I just wish I could trust my instincts and not second-guess everything. I mean, not everything needs to be this complicated, right?"

Samantha added, "I wish it didn't have to be. I wish I could just say what I'm thinking without worrying it's not good enough. But here we are."

"We're all in the same boat, I guess," Aradhana said. "It helps to know we're not alone."

Mia smiled. "For sure. It's nice to know we're all faking it in our own ways, together."

As they sipped the last of their chai, the table fell into a comfortable silence. Each friend reflected on their struggles, feeling a little less isolated and a little more understood.

Mia wondered if she'd ever have the courage to show her true self, unfiltered and unapologetic. Aarav considered how he could start making decisions without being paralyzed by doubt. Samantha thought about finding her voice and the strength to speak up in a world that often felt overwhelming. Aradhana resolved to find pride in her own achievements, regardless of comparisons. Meanwhile, Sidharth reflected on whether his relentless drive for success would ever fill the void of self-doubt. Though no solutions were found that evening, they took comfort in knowing they weren't alone in their struggles. As they gathered their things and prepared to leave, the unspoken bond between them strengthened, a shared understanding of the battles they faced within themselves.

With a wave and a promise to meet again, they stepped out into the evening, each carrying the weight of their reflections and the hope that tomorrow might bring new insights.

Self-esteem is a crucial element of our identity and plays a vital role in our mental and emotional well-being. It forms the foundation of our confidence and influences how we perceive ourselves in the world. Understanding the various types can help you identify which category you fall under:

1. **Low self-esteem is characterized by a negative self-view and a lack of confidence, often making individuals more susceptible to mental health concerns like depression and anxiety.**
2. **High self-esteem reflects a positive view of oneself and one's abilities,**

fostering confidence, resilience, and a strong sense of self-worth. People with high self-esteem are more likely to take risks and succeed in life.

3. Defensive self-esteem occurs when individuals, despite having high self-esteem, feel compelled to defend themselves and their abilities, leading to an unhealthy obsession with perfection and fear of failure.

4. Fragile self-esteem is another variant where high self-esteem is easily shaken by criticism or failure, resulting in defensiveness and a reluctance to take risks.

5. Healthy self-esteem, the ideal form, strikes a balance between confidence and humility, enabling individuals to have a positive view of themselves while recognising their limitations. Those with healthy self-esteem are open to feedback and able to handle setbacks gracefully.

1. What do you often second-guess about yourself, and why?

2. How does seeking external validation impact your decisions?

3. In what situations do you feel most confident and why?

4. What small step can you take today to trust your instincts more?

5. How can you support a friend who shares similar struggles with self-doubt?

Assurance

Breaking Out of the Cage

> *Remember, you have been criticizing yourself for years and it hasn't worked. Try approving of yourself and see what happens.*
>
> – *Louise L. Hay*

After a fruitful week at work, the group of friends gathered once again in the cozy corner of the office canteen. It was Friday evening, and they were ready to unwind and reflect on the past week.

Mia walked in with a big smile, "Guys, did you see Simone Biles at the Olympics? She was so adorable when she said, 'You got this!' to herself right before starting her routine. I couldn't stop thinking about what we talked about last time. Simone said, 'The hardest part after Tokyo is that I don't trust myself in gymnastics. And now I am choosing to wake up every day and remind myself that I can do this.' So powerful! It reminded me to keep in mind that social media isn't everything, even though I found THIS on social media." she laughed.

Aradhana smiled and nodded. "Mia, you find these gems. Also your creativity and the way you capture moments are truly unique. Honestly, I don't think anyone else sees the flaws you think you have. People admire the way you express yourself. Seriously, without your posts, our marketing campaign would be so blah!!"

Mia laughed, "Thanks, Aradhana. I needed to hear that."

Aarav turned to Aradhana, "You know, last time you mentioned feeling overshadowed by your brother, but honestly, I've always admired your dedication and attention to detail. Those are your superpowers, and they set you apart. I couldn't have run that project without you in the back end, making sure everything was spot-on."

Aradhana blushed, "Really? I always thought I needed to do more. But hey, if my superpowers include organizing chaos, I'll take it! Maybe you can tell my dad that—he still thinks I'm just sorting papers."

Samantha chimed in, "Aradhana, you have this incredible ability to see the big picture and the tiny details at the same time. That's something a lot of people can't do. I don't know how you keep everything straight while I'm still figuring out what's for lunch."

Aarav smiled, "Speaking of amazing abilities, Samantha, I know you sometimes doubt your voice, but your writing is so powerful. People don't see any flaws when they read your work; they see brilliance. Seriously, your emails are the only ones I don't dread opening."

Samantha grinned, "Thanks, Aarav. I'm working on speaking up more, but it helps to know my words are making an impact. And thanks for actually reading my emails instead of just pretending to!"

Sidharth raised his cup, "And Aarav, your instincts are spot on. I've seen how you handle operations, and I'm always impressed by your problem-solving skills. You worry about making the wrong choices, but everyone else sees your decisiveness and calm under pressure. Let's be real, I couldn't close a deal without you keeping everything running smoothly."

Aarav chuckled, "I appreciate that, Sidharth. I'm trying to trust myself more. I guess I'm like Batman, working in the shadows, except I'm afraid of making dinner plans."

Samantha turned to Sidharth, "You know, you always talk about being afraid to ask for help, but I see you as someone who lifts others up. You're a great leader, and that vulnerability you worry about? It makes you more relatable and strong. Plus, your sales pitches are legendary–you could probably sell ice to a polar bear!"

Sidharth laughed, "Thanks, guys. I'm learning that I don't have to carry everything alone. And trust me, that polar bear deal is next on my list!"

Mia added, "Seriously though, it seems easy to just be confident, but it's terrifying sometimes. I wish the boss would see that too."

"Right?" Aradhana chimed in. "Maybe if we all tell my dad how awesome I am, he'll finally give me that car I've been asking for."

The group burst into laughter, enjoying the lighthearted banter. But as the laughter subsided, Samantha's eyes welled up with tears. "It's just... hearing you all say these things, it means a lot. I've been so hard on myself."

According to Sociometer Theory, developed by Mark Leary, self-esteem acts as a social indicator rather than just a desire for positive self-evaluation. This theory suggests that we have an internal 'sociometer' that gauges our social standing and reflects how accepted or valued we feel by others.

Self-concept is a combination of what I think of myself, what others think of me, and what I think others think of me. Self-esteem arises when we start making comparisons, as we tend to measure ourselves against other people. We have a need to feel connected and accepted by our environment, which influences our self-perception.

Our self-esteem will depend on our thought processes and the feedback we receive from those around us. However, what ultimately trumps all of this is our own perception, our tendency to compare ourselves, and the core beliefs

formed during early childhood. These experiences shape our fundamental views about ourselves.

Recognising these core beliefs is important. If they are healthy, self-esteem becomes less reliant on external validation because a strong self-concept fosters internal confidence and stability.

Aarav reached over and squeezed her hand. "Hey, we've got your back. We all need reminders sometimes."

Sidharth nodded, "Yeah, Sam. We see how incredible you are, even if you don't always see it yourself."

Samantha wiped her tears and smiled. "You know, I talked to my mom about all this last night. She said tackling low self-esteem is like embarking on an epic solo road trip to discover who you really are. Complete with scenic routes, unexpected detours, and yes, even a few flat tires along the way. It's about acknowledging every part of the journey–the smooth rides and the bumpy roads—and finding a sense of peace in the whole chaotic adventure. She told me it's about realising who you are and who you're not, and being okay with both."

Aradhana nodded thoughtfully, "Your mom sounds wise. It really is about the journey, isn't it?"

Mia added, "Yes, and the fact that we're all in it together makes it less scary."

The group fell silent for a moment, letting the weight of their support settle in. It was a reminder that they weren't alone in their struggles and that together, they could face anything.

An important understanding of self assurance lies in accepting the different parts of who we are. It's only when we give recognition to our strengths and acknowledge our weaknesses, do we truly take the responsibility of being us. Self-esteem lies in accepting who we are, including our insufficiencies and yet actively choosing to like ourselves.

Mia added, "Yeah, and the fact that we're all in it together makes it less scary."

Sidharth leaned forward, "So, if we're taking this solo road trip, who else do we need to bring along?."

Aarav grinned hesitantly, "Well, maybe awareness to begin with? That little lightbulb moment when you realize, 'Hey, it's time to sort this out.'"

Mia nodded, "Awareness is key in most things! One has to first recognise that low self-esteem doesn't have to be the boss of you—it's just one part of your story, not the entire narrative. It's sitting with those moments of doubt and gently reminding yourself, 'The show isn't over yet!'"

Aradhana added, "Right. It's knowing that we are so much more than the little bits. As they say, "Whole is bigger than the sum of its parts". That you have more than the things that you are not good at and all the things that you fear. There is more to you as a human being beyond your flaws and even your achievements."

Samantha chimed in, "But what about self-doubt?"

Aradhana continued, "It's about being okay with not having all the answers right now and acknowledging the uncertainties and the uncomfortable bits. Self-doubt might not be the friend we asked for, but instead of pushing it away, we can learn a lot by sitting down with it and understanding its layers."

Self-doubt often leads to emotional dysregulation, where negative thoughts and feelings make it challenging to manage and respond flexibly to our emotions. This can leave us feeling overwhelmed and impulsive, with frequent mood swings and a tendency towards perfectionism. An intriguing concept in Dialectical Behaviour Therapy focuses on reducing emotional vulnerability. The key components of this approach include practicing active self-care, intentionally

increasing pleasant events and positive experiences rather than waiting for them to happen, and building awareness of our values and life goals, taking actionable steps toward achieving them. Overcoming self-doubt is our responsibility.

Sidharth smiled, "And finally patience—taking the time to really explore who you are, what makes you tick, what sparks joy, and what triggers those doubts. It's in these moments of introspection that you'll find the keys to unlocking self-acceptance. You know patience pays in a great many ways!"

Aarav laughed, "And for everything else, there's the 'Fake it till you make it' strategy, right?"

They all chuckled, feeling a renewed sense of camaraderie and understanding. The conversation had shifted from focusing solely on their flaws to embracing the journey of self-discovery, together and with a little help from their metaphorical travel companions.

As they finished their chai and prepared to leave, they felt lighter, knowing they had each other and the tools they needed for the journey ahead. With a wave and a promise to keep supporting one another, they stepped out into the evening, ready to tackle whatever challenges lay ahead, one mile at a time. As they finished their chai, they left the canteen with renewed confidence and a commitment to lift each other up. With a wave and a promise to keep supporting one another, they stepped out into the evening, ready to tackle whatever challenges lay ahead.

The Johari Window, developed by psychologists Joseph Luft and Harrington Ingham, proposes an interesting way to understand how we perceive ourselves and how much of that comes from within us vs from other people.

It consists of 4 quadrants:

1. **Open Area: The things about us that we know and everyone else knows.**
2. **Hidden Area: The things about us that we are aware of, but others aren't.**
3. **Blind Area: The things about us that others are aware of, but we aren't.**
4. **Unknown Area: The things about us that both ourselves and others are unaware of.**

Through personal reflection and conversations with others in our lives, we can fill in our personal Johari Window to understand, truly, who we are and how we are perceived.

1. Who are the "companions" you rely on during your own journey of self-discovery, and how do they help you navigate challenges?

2. What are some "scenic routes" in your life where you've discovered unexpected strengths or joys?

3. How can you practice patience and self-awareness when facing self-doubt, and what strategies can help you overcome it?

4. In what areas of your life do you find yourself 'faking it', and how can you work towards authenticity and self-acceptance?

5. How can you support others in their journey to build self-esteem and confidence, and how does this support reflect on your own growth?

Regret

Learning

8

Regret

Echoes From the Past

> ***Regret is such a short word and yet, it stretches on forever.***
>
> *– Ranata Suzuki*

The argument between her husband and daughter reverberated through the house like a storm, leaving chaos in its wake. As she attempted to mediate, their words seemed to bounce off her, and the conflict felt insurmountable. "You don't understand anything!" they both screamed at her. It was one of those days when an existential crisis set in, making her question everything she had sacrificed for this family. Why did I give up everything for this? she thought, feeling the weight of her choices press down on her. In the aftermath, she looked back at what, in the moment, seemed like a trash heap of memories—fragments of a life filled with missed opportunities and unfulfilled ambitions.

"Could I have been the school principal?" Sushma wondered aloud, her voice a mix of longing and lament. At 50, her career felt like a series of missed exits on a highway she once drove with ambition. As she sifted through memories of choices made, a particular kind of sorrow settled in—the kind that comes from knowing you've closed doors on yourself, some of which led to places you can only now imagine. She realized that she had not taken the courses and certifications that qualified her for the position. She yearned for the respect that came with the designation and couldn't make peace looking at her grown children and her beautiful home, things she was proud of otherwise. She had had to choose to raise her children or devote time to another certification. There was a yearning to turn back time, rewrite the script, and change things just a little. But at 50, with retirement around the corner, the ink has dried, and the story remains unwritten and incomplete.

Her life had been a series of choices, some dictated by circumstance and others by the heart. The decision to focus on family had been one she never questioned until now. When her first child was born, she decided to stay home, nurturing and guiding her children through their formative years. Her days were filled with laughter, school projects, and the gentle chaos that only children can bring. She had learned the hard way that the best way to be appreciated in the family was to not be there sometimes. As the years passed, however, she watched her colleagues climb the professional ladder while she balanced the roles of mother, wife, and occasional substitute teacher.

She wondered about the other dreams she left behind—not just the career milestones but the adventures she had envisioned in her youth. Travel plans postponed, fitness goals unmet, and hobbies abandoned all echoed in the corridors of her mind, reminding her of roads not taken. There were moments she longed to see the world beyond her immediate horizon, to challenge herself physically and mentally in ways that only seemed possible before life's responsibilities took hold.

Consider that moment when you made a choice, and in hindsight, it was evidently not the wisest one. For instance, the job you didn't apply for because you felt underqualified. Years later, you might look back and wonder what could have transpired if you had seized that opportunity. You also see your colleagues who were ambitious enough to risk it and

how their careers developed. Or perhaps it was a past relationship where unspoken words left you pondering the potential that could have flourished had you spoken up. You remained single and infatuated while the other person moved on and is now nurturing their family. Or the poor financial decisions of overspending, accumulating debt, or neglecting savings for the future. Your friend has a house while you have expensive restaurant bills and clothes you can no longer fit into! The list is endless.

Life is about playing the odds, and we all think about the odds differently. It's like that old college sweater you can't bring yourself to throw away. It doesn't fit, it's hopelessly out of fashion, and let's be honest, it's seen better days. Yet, there it hangs, a testament to what once was. The best classification and framework to understand regret was offered by Daniel Pink, the author of *The Power of Regret: How Looking Backward Moves Us Forward.* He classifies regrets in four buckets:

Consider, for instance, the **foundational regrets.** These are the bricks and mortar of the House of Hindsight. "If only I'd saved a bit more money," we lament while staring wistfully at a bank statement that seems to mock us with its meager figures. Or, "If only I'd studied a bit harder," as we watch our peers ascend the glittering rungs of success while we remain firmly on the ground floor. It's as if life were a game of Monopoly and we'd spent all our time in jail, watching others pass Go and collect $200.

Then there are the **boldness regrets**, the paths not taken because we were too timid to set foot upon them. "If only I'd taken that job in Outer Mongolia," we muse, ignoring the fact that at the time, the thought of Mongolian winters made us shiver more than the prospect of adventure. Or, "If only I'd asked Arjun out," conveniently forgetting that back then, we had the romantic appeal of a wet sock and the confidence of a meek squirrel.

Moral regrets are perhaps the trickiest of the lot. They're the smudges on our conscience that no amount of rationalizing can erase. "If only I hadn't told that lie," we think, as though admitting it now, in the solitude of our minds, might absolve us of the deed. It's akin to returning to the scene of a crime and hoping the statute of limitations has passed. Unfortunately, our conscience is a relentless detective, immune to such legal niceties.

Connection regrets, on the other hand, are all about the bridges we've burned or failed to build. "If only I'd kept in touch with old what's-their-name," we sigh, scrolling through social media profiles of people whose lives seem to have progressed without us. It's a bit like discovering a party to which we were never invited, hosted by someone we once knew when the world was younger and our social circles less circular.

Having learned about the four different kinds of regret—foundational regrets, boldness regrets, moral regrets, and connection regrets—think back to your own experiences.

Can you identify which type of regret resonates most with your own experiences? Can you recall specific instances in your life that align with each category and how these regrets influenced your thoughts and actions?

In the end, regret is a curious beast. It's an emotion that manages to be both exquisitely personal and utterly universal. We all have our catalogue of could-haves and should-haves, each as unique as a fingerprint and as common as the cold. But here's the crux of the matter: without regret, would we ever learn? Would we ever grow? It's the pebble in our shoe that reminds us to watch our step, the gentle nudge not to make the same mistake twice.

As the day drew to a close, Sushma found herself sitting on the swing in her living room, a cup of tea in hand, watching the sun dip below the horizon. She decided to write a letter to her younger self. She would present this to her daughter on her 18th birthday next year with the hope of passing on her learnings from her life.

Do you like to take the opportunities that come your way, or do you play it safe? Close your eyes and feel the sting of a past mistake. Does it gnaw at you with self-blame, or does it stir a yearning to change the past? Let's explore this internal battle.

1. What is one regret that still lingers in your mind, and how can you transform it into a lesson for the future?

2. When faced with a choice, how do you ensure that your decision aligns with your long-term values and goals?

3. How do you navigate the tension between personal aspirations and responsibilities to others?

4. How have you used past regrets to fuel positive changes in your life?

5. What is one bold step you can take today to create a future with fewer regrets?

Learning

Looking back to move forward

> “*No amount of regret changes the past, no amount of anxiety changes the future. But any amount of gratitude changes the present.*”
>
> *– Marc and Angel Chernoff*

Regret is an emotion we all encounter at various points in our lives. It's that nagging feeling that whispers “what if?” as we reflect on decisions made and paths not taken. While regret can often seem like a heavy burden, it also holds the potential to be a powerful teacher. By embracing regret, we can turn past mistakes into stepping stones for growth and self-discovery.

Here's the letter Sushma wrote for her daughter.

Dear Stuti,

Happy 18th Birthday! I can hardly believe you're officially an adult now. It feels like just yesterday you were learning to ride a bike and accidentally crashing into the rose bushes in our garden. As you step into this new chapter of your life, I wanted to share some thoughts on a topic that has often kept me up at night—regret. Not because I want to dampen your day but because I think it might help you on your own path with a bit more clarity and maybe save you from making some of the same mistakes I did.

Regret is one of those emotions that everyone experiences, whether it's regretting wearing socks with sandals or something a bit more serious. But it's also something that can teach us a lot, as long as we let it. Imagine regret as that friend who's brutally honest with you, telling you when you have spinach stuck in your teeth or when you've made a poor choice. It can be uncomfortable, but it's also super helpful in the long run.

Years ago, I met this wise man from a village in Rajasthan. He was an Ashoka Fellow and did amazing work conserving forests. He told me something that stuck with me: "We often dwell on the could-haves and would-haves, but the price we paid was the lesson we refused to learn."

As for me, I've had my fair share of regrets—like not becoming a school principal. Sometimes I wonder if I should have pursued that path. You know, there's something appealing about having a plaque with my name on it. Instead, I chose to focus on our family, and while I cherish every moment with you and your dad,

I occasionally catch myself daydreaming about that alternate reality where I'm the big boss at a school.

Remember that time I tried to make a family dinner and ended up with a kitchen disaster? I regretted not taking those cooking classes back in the day. But we learned to laugh about it (and always have a pizza delivery number on hand).

I'm writing this today because, on your special day, I want to remind you that regrets are not the end of the world. They're more like guideposts, reminding us of the choices we've made and nudging us to make better ones in the future. And yes, sometimes they remind us to avoid my kitchen experiments.

To help you understand this better, I've got you a book as a birthday gift: If Only ... Finding Freedom From Regret by Robert Leahy, PhD. It talks about how regret can be productive or unproductive. Productive regret is like when you realize you've watched an entire season of a show in one night, but it pushes you to set some boundaries next time. Unproductive regret, though, is when you just sit there, binge-watching the next season with no lesson learned.

In life, you'll find that people regret things they didn't do more often than the things they did. Some folks regret not taking that job, going on that trip, or telling someone how they really feel. So, my advice to you, dear daughter, is to be brave, fearless and experimental. Don't be afraid to make mistakes. Just learn from them.

As you celebrate this milestone birthday, remember that it's okay to make choices that don't work out as planned. What matters is how you use those experiences to grow and improve. Embrace your adventures, take risks, and if you do stumble, know that it's all part of the journey. And always keep a sense of humor about it—life is too short to take ourselves too seriously.

I love you more than words can say, and I'm so proud of the young woman you've become. Here's to an amazing future filled with lessons, laughter, and lots of love.

With all my heart,

Mom

Regret is about a fictional world—a counterfactual world. It's about possibilities rather than facts. It involves imagining what could be instead of living in the real world and making the best of what we have. This perspective doesn't mean resignation or giving up; it means striving for better outcomes while appreciating our current circumstances.

Culturally, people tend to regret actions not taken, such as pursuing a course of education or forming a relationship. These regrets linger as unpleasant feelings, leading to rumination for months, years, or decades. Interestingly, research indicates that men have more regrets about achievement and materialism, while women have regrets about relationships and intimacy. Cultural differences show that Americans tend to regret romance, education, and career, while people in Asian cultures often regret family and interpersonal relationships.

Serenity and joy comes when you learn to embrace the roles you are destined to play and learn from the parts you did not get to play. Productive regret involves the ability to learn from mistakes or to anticipate learning from future missteps. It prompts self-correction and positive change.

1. Can you identify a moment in your life where you experienced regret? How has this experience shaped your choices and perspective since then?

2. Would you like to reframe past mistakes as opportunities for growth and learning? What lessons can you extract from them to inform your future decisions?

3. What fears have held you back from pursuing certain opportunities, and how can you overcome them to embrace new challenges with courage?

4. Think of a time when someone shared their regrets or life lessons with you. How did this influence your own approach to decision-making?

5. What steps can you take to live more authentically and make decisions aligned with your values, reducing the likelihood of future regrets?

Betrayal

Discernment

9

Betrayal

The Lingering Shadow of Broken Trust

> ***"Nothing hurts more than being disappointed by the single person you thought would never hurt you."***
>
> *– Gugu Mofokeng*

We sat with this chapter for a very long time. After our initial notes, it took us a few weeks and countless iterations to churn out the first draft. We then revisited it, discussing further, and once again. With every discussion and bit of research, an avalanche of emotions emerged.

What do you do when you realize that someone you love has cheated on you, stabbed you in the back, stolen from you, or lied to you? The partner who did not show up on the wedding day? The parent who kept quiet when their child shared about sexual abuse? The manager who takes money on the side without reporting it and misuses their power? Have you been there? What did you feel?

Avantika and John had a beautiful, multicultural wedding—six years of dating each other and blissful togetherness. The festivities began with a vibrant mehendi ceremony, a playful cricket match between the boys' side and the girls' side, and a ceremony that promised eternal togetherness. As the euphoria of the festivities waned, they retired to their room as a newlywed couple. The next morning, as they woke up, Avantika said, "Good morning, my love! ! I can't believe we are finally husband and wife!"

John replied with a pale face, "I made a mistake last night! I didn't want to get married!" He watched Avantika's reaction and quickly laughed, "Pulling your leg Avi! Come let's have breakfast."

She laughed nervously, brushing it off, believing him and that he was joking about random things. They had been together for six years, and he had proposed. She was mentally not ready to get married. Little did Avantika know, this was not just said in jest. The realization dawned on her a few days later during their wedding reception, through a mere glance exchanged between John and Aditi, a new friend he recently made on Twitter. This glance made Avantika realize that she was unwittingly the third wheel in her own relationship. A wave of nausea hit her at that moment. Her heart pounded in her chest, each beat echoing the painful truth she had just uncovered. Her mouth went dry, and she felt a cold sweat break out across her back. The joyous atmosphere of the wedding reception faded into a blur, replaced by a feeling she could not understand. Avantika's mind raced, replaying moments from their past, searching for signs she had missed. Anger and hurt surged through her, mingling with disbelief. Was she imagining things? Was she just thinking too much of the situation? She felt a hollow ache in her chest, a void left by the shattering of her once secure world.

As they drove home from the reception, just the two of them in the car, John smiled at her and said, "I found a new song. Wanna hear it?" She smiled back and the song came on. Songs were their common love language and often how they communicated. She was comforted by the gesture. The artist began singing ...

"Now and then I think of when we were together
Like when you said you felt so happy you could die
Told myself that you were right for me
But felt so lonely in your company
But that was love, and it's an ache I still remember

Now you're just somebody that I used to know
Somebody (I used to know)
Somebody (now you're just somebody that I used to know)
Somebody (I used to know)
Somebody (now you're just somebody that I used to know)
I used to know
That I used to know I used to know
Somebody"

Avantika knew what John was saying in an instance. It was like she was punched in her stomach!

The subsequent months were painful, to say the least, John would neither accept nor deny this new reality. She did not confront him or ask him, she just chose to observe. He would be a loving husband and then pull away, pretending to be busy. He began taking more work trips and being apart from Avantika more often. When he was in the city, he would not express love like he did before. He refused to touch her. Each time he left, she felt a piece of her heart crumble. The inconsistency and mixed signals only added to Avantika's pain. She felt like she was living in a constant state of confusion and doubt. The person she had trusted with her life seemed like a stranger now, and each day was a struggle to make sense of what was happening. Her mind was a whirlwind of thoughts, replaying every moment of their relationship, searching for clues she might have overlooked. She had loved John with every fiber of her being, and the idea that he might have been unfaithful felt like a punch to the gut. Despite her suspicions, she couldn't bring herself to confront him directly. Instead, she found herself caught in a web of uncertainty, her heart torn between the love she still felt and the betrayal that seemed to lurk beneath the surface.

Avantika tried to maintain a brave face, but inside, she was unraveling. She questioned her worth, wondering what she had done wrong and why she wasn't enough for John. The constant emotional rollercoaster left her exhausted, yet she clung to the hope that things might somehow return to the way they were. She couldn't understand how someone who had promised her forever could also be the source of such deep heartache. The man she had known for six years, who had whispered sweet promises of a shared future, was now a puzzle she couldn't solve.

After a few months, Avantika couldn't take it anymore and confronted John. While he kept dodging for a while, he finally admitted that he was not sure about the marriage anymore and had feelings for Aditi. It became clear to Avantika that there was no future, and the short marriage turned into a long, drawn out separation. After months of pain, the ordeal ended in a divorce.

John and Aditi married a year later in a small cozy wedding and moved to another country.

The months turned into years, and while the pain of betrayal never fully left her, Avantika learned to live with it. She threw herself into her work, finding comfort in the routines that kept her mind occupied. On the surface, she appeared strong and composed, but deep down, the scars of John's betrayal lingered.

Avantika was haunted by questions. Why hadn't John spoken up during their year-long engagement, or even the day before their wedding? They could have parted ways quietly, without the spectacle that it turned into, humiliating both their families. And why invite Aditi to their wedding? Was there anything Avantika could have done to prevent this? The months that followed felt as if she was hit by a bomb, seeing her limbs disengaged from her body.

The initial shock can be paralysing, making it hard to breathe, or think. It feels like the ground beneath one's feet has disappeared, leaving them in a free fall of disbelief and pain. The betrayal cuts deep, turning trust into ashes and leaving wounds that don't easily heal. One might feel anger, a burning rage that makes them want to lash out, to hurt the betrayer as much as they have been hurt. At times, there might be a feeling of numbness, as if emotions have been switched off, leaving an empty void where there used to be love and warmth.

Betrayal, by its very nature, feels deeply personal, often leading to a cynical view of trust and the motivations of others. It causes a kind of mental contamination, one that permeates many areas of our life. It's grief. It's a loss. It's anger. It's mistrust. It's hopelessness. It's helplessness.

The analogy of betrayal being akin to termites eating away at a cupboard is particularly apt. On the surface, everything appears functional—sturdy, even. But inside, the integrity of the structure is compromised, weakened by countless, unseen cracks. Betrayal infects our mental landscape quietly but destructively. It eats away at our foundational beliefs about loyalty, integrity, and trust. This mental contamination leaves us questioning the solidity of our other relationships and our capacity to judge character, making us wonder if what we see is truly what we get or if there's another layer of decay beneath the surface.

This contamination is so destabilising because we make the choice to include somebody in our life with the hope of feeling safe with them. We let them into our mind, our heart, our being—trusting that they will treat our vulnerable selves with care and respect. When we are betrayed, we feel a sense of deep loss. It feels like an erosion; a corruption of the way we view ourselves, our lives, and the world around us.

One evening, as Avantika sat watching Game of Thrones, the infamous Red Wedding episode unfolded before her eyes. When she saw the shock and betrayal portrayed on screen, it seemed no different to her than what happened to her own self. The death of part of the well-meaning Stark family took her back to her experience- the destruction of the future she hoped for, through no fault of her own.

After that, Avantika found herself drawn to movies that explored themes of betrayal. Watching Gone Girl, she felt a pang of recognition in the twisted, deceitful narrative. The suspense and emotional turmoil mirrored her own feelings of confusion and hurt.

In these moments, Avantika realised that it's easier to accept evil from evil, but very difficult to accept betrayal from a person you entrust with safety. These stories, though fictional, provided a strange comfort, helping her process the layers of her own experience. "Et tu, Brute?" she often thought, the phrase echoing in her mind as she continued her journey of healing.

1. Avantika trusted John implicitly, only to have that trust shattered. How do you think your worldview would change after an incident like the one that happened with Avantika?

2. Explore the emotional journey Avantika undergoes—from shock and disbelief to anger, numbness, and eventually a quieter, enduring pain. Why do these emotions evolve and persist long after the initial betrayal?

3. Avantika's experience highlights how betrayal can lead to questioning one's worth and identity. Have you had moments in your own life where betrayal has made you question who you are and what you deserve?

4. How does forgiveness—or the lack thereof—affect your ability to move forward after a betrayal?

Discernment

The Quiet Power of Knowing What Truly Matters

> ***Discernment is not knowing the difference between right and wrong. It is knowing the difference between right and almost right.***
>
> ***– Charles Spurgeon***

Healing from betrayal is as much about cleaning the termite-infested cupboard as it is about rebuilding it stronger and more resilient than before. It's a process of acknowledging the pain and the breach of trust while also engaging in the slow, meticulous work of repairing our sense of safety and our ability to trust. This journey is deeply personal and varies from one individual to another, but it always starts with the self—rebuilding self-esteem, reasserting self-worth, and gradually restoring faith in the goodness of others.

As one takes this journey, one needs a new life skill, that of discernment. Discernment is a skill that allows one to see things for what they really are and not what we want them to be. As the famous preacher Charles Spurgeon said, "Discernment is not knowing the difference between what is right or wrong. It is knowing the difference between right and almost right." It is a form of learned emotional intelligence where we learn to make a distinction between two things that might seem similar. Let's go back to Avantika's story.

While John played the perfect husband every few days, it was important for Avantika to see things in perspective and understand that there was more to the story than met the eye. The act of betrayal challenged her to differentiate between the deliberate intention and the natural end of a relationship, where both parties were genuine but ultimately not aligned.

Dr. Debi Sibler has done three decades of research on this topic and runs the Post Betrayal Trauma Institute in the US. She has created a five-step framework that helps one deal with betrayal and move forward in life. Just like grief and the stages one goes through, in the case of betrayal, one also goes through five stages. We may not face these stages sequentially and may stay on a particular stage for a brief period.

Stage I: Set-Up Stage

Think of it as a table with four legs—physical, emotional, spiritual, and mental. These legs have been dismantled, and you will need all four for the table to stand again.

In the initial days after discovering John's betrayal, Avantika felt as if the foundation of her life had been ripped apart. Her once solid table of existence now lay in pieces. She experienced a physical exhaustion that sleep couldn't cure, an emotional numbness that left her feeling detached, a spiritual crisis where she questioned her faith, and a mental fog that clouded her thoughts. It was as if every aspect of her being had been dismantled.

Stage II: Shock and Trauma

"I was going in a safe boat. How did my boat start sinking? This doesn't happen to people like us."

This stage involves the breakdown of the body, mind, and worldview. The mental model that protects you is shattered, and this is your bottom but not the rock bottom.

Avantika vividly remembered the moment the realization hit her. The world around her seemed to blur, sounds became distant, and she felt as if she were free-falling into an abyss. She couldn't fathom how her safe and predictable life had turned into a nightmare. Her body reacted with shaking hands and a racing heart, her mind couldn't process the betrayal, and her view of the world and the people in it was irrevocably altered. She questioned everything she had believed about love, loyalty, and trust.

Stage III: Survival Instincts

This stage is a bit like the notorious line from Hotel California by The Eagles "You can check out anytime you like, but you can never leave."

By this point, you have probably come to terms with the fact that you were betrayed – but it is still too painful to face the full depth of the emotions it made you feel. You may take pleasure in your newfound functionality – the ability to move out of a constant state of numbness and pain and do the things that need doing. You tell people about what happened and everyone instantly takes your side, comforting you and even banding with you to point to all the ways that the perpetrator did you wrong. Your functionality may rely on a constant supply of instantly gratifying behaviour like emotional eating, using drugs, alcohol. As long as you don't get the time to think, everything seems all right.

It may not feel like it, but this state is like being in limbo. You're able to go about your day better than before, but your life still is an endless loop of coping strategies that don't end up helping you get out of that loop. This is where many people get stuck, thinking that true healing has occurred. But the journey still remains.

In the months that followed, Avantika threw herself into her work, using it as a shield against the pain. She became fiercely independent, refusing help from friends and family. "I can handle this," she would tell herself. But deep down, she knew she was stuck in survival mode. She found small comforts in being right, in directing her anger at John, and in the sympathy she garnered from those who knew her story. Yet, this wasn't true healing. She realized she was numbing herself with work, avoiding the deeper emotional work needed to move forward. The longer she stayed in this space, the more it felt like she was trapped in a never-ending cycle of pain and self-deception.

Stage IV: Finding and Adjusting to a New Normal

"I cannot control what happened, but I can choose to do what takes me forward."

This decision will be a key moment that brings you firmly into the territory of healing and acceptance. The decision will never be easy – you will find yourself going back and forth between this stage and the last, and it will take a lot of strength to let go of the memories. Think of it like moving to a new house and leaving behind things that don't serve your new purpose. It's always hard to do that, you wonder if you will ever need those things again. But how do you make that choice? You sit down and assess whether you actually need them, whether they will serve a purpose in your new house, your new life. Sometimes, instead of leaving things behind entirely, you put them all into a little cardboard box to give them a new meaning in your new life – a reminder of what you went through and learned from. Other times, you enlist the help of people who are close to you, who can provide you with a more objective sense of what you would actually need.

This is the same way in which you make the decision to move forward from difficult feelings. You discard, repurpose, make new meaning, and rely on social support. You realize that you are not just a sum of the things you went through, but also how you found your way through them. The turning point is the same – when you finally realize that there exists a choice to move forward, one you CAN make, it gives you a sense of renewed hope. Rebuilding trust involves making healthy decisions for yourself, part of which is finding non-judgmental resources that can support you through the process.

For Avantika, this meant seeking support from her lawyer and psychologist to move through this phase in her life.

She decided to leave behind everything that reminded her of the betrayal—old photos, gifts, and even certain mutual friends. She got a scholarship in a masters' program and moved to a small town in Europe. It was a slow process, but she began to rebuild her life. Therapy, sports, music, the company of strangers, who didn't judge her and could offer practical advice on moving forward, helped in her healing. She learned to make decisions based on what was healthy for her, gradually restoring her ability to trust.

Stage V: Healing and Rebirth

As the pain begins to heal, you establish new boundaries and a fresh worldview. Your physical and mental healing becomes more grounded, paving the way for spiritual and emotional recovery. Spiritual healing involves reconnecting with yourself and finding a way to embrace who you are now, after all the changes and experiences you've undergone. It's a shift in energy that transforms how you perceive yourself and the world around you.

Emotional healing is about self-acceptance and compassion. It involves integrating the new reality that life has presented and gradually becoming comfortable with it. It's the process of incorporating all the heavy emotions that once held you back into a space where your soul releases toxic feelings and is ready to step out in a new form. It's like finally feeling settled in a new neighborhood. This stage brings new levels of health and relationships, and a rebirth of ideas and emotions. A stronger, healthier version of yourself emerges with a renewed sense of belonging.

Feeling psychologically safe is crucial for human development; without it, integrating yourself into your environment becomes difficult. You learn to activate different parts of yourself—whether fearful, hurt, or trusting—depending on what is needed at the moment.

As she embraced this new phase of her life, Avantika felt a subtle transformation. She established new boundaries, ensuring that her relationships were based on mutual respect and trust. Her physical and mental health improved as she prioritised self-care and personal growth. Spiritually and emotionally, she found peace and began to heal from the wounds of the past. Avantika emerged as a stronger, healthier version of herself. She discovered new passions and rebuilt her social circle with people who uplifted and supported her. The betrayal no longer defined her; it became a part of her story that led to her rebirth.

As the personal development coach Dr. Debi Silber beautifully describes, think of what you had as an incredible creation of Lego pieces. And then it just fell apart. The pile of Lego pieces, destroyed, sits there, but you have the option to build something new and more beautiful with it.

Understanding betrayal requires a nuanced view of human nature, the dynamics of relationships, and our own vulnerabilities and strengths. Sometimes, it's the chasm between expectations and reality which label an action as 'betrayal'. This differentiation is crucial in managing the aftermath of betrayal, including the mental contamination and psychological unsafety it can evoke.

Reflecting on betrayal thus becomes a prompt not just for navigating personal trauma but for a broader contemplation on how we view the world and our place within it. It's an invitation to assess our sensitivity, tolerance, and the psychological flexibility needed to face life's inevitable challenges without losing our capacity for trust, love, and hope.

People like to talk about discernment but often do not act on it. Discernment is a decision-making process that honours the place of God's will in our lives. It involves prayer, scripture, tradition, and experience - weighing facts and feelings, and discerning the best choice about what fits you most.

One has to be attentive to false consolations. Often, the desperation for connection, trust, and vulnerability or just plain greed leads to overlooking potential red flags, driven by an inherent need for belonging, love, or a handsome return on what we may have invested.

Avantika, too, had to navigate through these stages. Initially paralyzed by the shock and trauma of John's betrayal, she slowly moved towards survival instincts, relying solely on herself. But she realized this was not a place to stay forever. With time, she began finding a new normal, understanding that she could not control what had happened but could control her path forward. She built new relationships based on trust and respect, choosing to let go of those who did not serve her new purpose.

It's taken over a decade for Avantika to move past some pieces of her trauma, and the journey is still ongoing. She is continuously learning to apply these principles in all areas of her life.

1. Consider how Avantika's initial shock and trauma stemmed from the disconnect between her expectations of John as a husband and the reality of his actions. Reflect on situations in your own life where expectations have influenced your perception of betrayal.

2. How can developing discernment help distinguish between genuine trustworthiness and potential betrayal? Think about times in your own life when improved discernment could have changed the outcome of a situation involving trust.

3. Explore the five stages of healing described by Dr. Debi Sibler and reflect on Avantika's journey through these stages. How do these stages relate to your own experiences of personal growth through adversity?

4. Avantika initially relied heavily on herself during the survival instincts stage. Reflect on the tension between independence and seeking support in times of crisis. How can finding this balance contribute to healing and rebuilding trust in yourself and others?

5. Think about Avantika's journey from idealising her marriage to questioning fundamental beliefs about love and loyalty. Reflect on your own beliefs about these concepts and how experiences of betrayal might challenge or reinforce them. How can we maintain hope and trust despite experiencing betrayal?

Guilt

Acceptance

10

Guilt

The Silent Burden

> *Guilt is the price we pay willingly for doing what we are going to do anyway.*
>
> *– Isabelle Holland*

In the dining room's gentle glow, a feeling of warmth wraps around the family as they come together at the table. This weekly dinner, a pause in their bustling lives, is a treasured ritual of unity and bonding. Here, amidst the carefully set table, it transforms into more than just mealtime; it's a refuge where stories flow, laughter resonates, and even tears are welcomed.

Tonight, however, was a little different. The tantalising aroma of Yasha's famous mutton biryani wafted through the air, hinting at comfort, yet there was a noticeable tension simmering just beneath the surface. Yasha, ever the perceptive sister, looked at her brother Ashwin, who was fiddling with the playlist and decided it was time to address the elephant in the room – Ashwin's emotional turmoil.

"Ashwin, how have you been holding up?" Yasha's voice was gentle but insistent, like a feather duster that had decided today was the day to tackle the cobwebs in the corners of her brother's heart. Ashwin's partner Aidan had had an overdose and was rushed to the hospital a few weeks ago.

Ashwin looked up, his eyes meeting Yasha's for the briefest of moments before darting back to his plate. "I've been...fine," he mumbled, though the word 'fine' felt as convincing as a silent orchestra.

The room fell silent, save for the music in the background. Their parents exchanged worried glances, silently urging Ashwin to open up.

"Ashwin, we're worried about you," Yasha pressed on, her tone firm but loving. "And we're worried about Aidan too."

The mention of Aidan's name seemed to snap Ashwin out of his trance. He was instantly transported to that moment a week ago, when at a party there was sudden panic with Aidan sprawled out on the bathroom floor, unconscious. The terror he felt that day almost lived in his body now. Finding Aidan in that state was a shock that spurred him into action- he rushed to check on him, relieved to find a pulse. He called an ambulance, called both their families, and made sure Aidan got the help he needed within the next 30 minutes. What words could communicate the horror of that incident?

Back at the dinner table, he took a deep breath, his shoulders slumping under the weight of unsaid words. "I noticed Aidan was struggling," he began, his voice barely above a whisper. "But I didn't say anything. I was afraid of pushing him away. I thought...maybe he'd sort it out himself."

Ashwin shared how he wakes up in the middle of the night drenched in sweat, unable to come to terms with what if Aidan had not reached the hospital in time. He loved Aidan and cared deeply for him. Ashwin could never convince Aidan to not consume drugs at a party. Over the years alcohol and drugs became the center of their evenings.

Ashwin's guilt was palpable. He carried a psychological burden—a persistent anxiety that constantly nagged at him, telling him he could have acted sooner. His inner critic relentlessly questioned him: "Why didn't you say something? If you had spoken up or done something, maybe Aiden wouldn't have ended up in rehab. Are you the reason for his excessive drinking and experimenting?

He wasn't like that before he met you." Ashwin was overwhelmed with guilt and felt responsible for what happened to Aidan, as if it was his fault, even if it was unintentional.

My guilt tells me that what I did was not okay. This self-conscious emotion makes me feel morally wrong or responsible. Guilt is a complex emotion because each of us has our own moral standards and values that guide how we want to live and conduct ourselves. However, when we fall short, it leaves us with a deep, uncomfortable feeling of distress about our wrongdoing, whether real or imagined. Think about a time when you felt guilty. What triggered that feeling? How did it impact you, and how did you respond?

A heavy silence settled over the table. Ashwin's guilt was a living thing, clawing at his insides, reminding him of every moment he had chosen silence over confrontation. It gnawed at him, relentless and unforgiving. "Had we not reached the hospital in time the other day... !" he trailed off and sighed. The heaviness of guilt was like carrying a stone in his chest, one that pressed down with each beat of his heart. It whispered insidiously that he should have done more, could have been more, and that perhaps his efforts were too little, too late. Ashwin felt trapped in a cycle of self-blame, where the past seemed unchangeable, yet the desire to rewrite it was overwhelming.

Ashwin and Aidan met in the most unexpected of places—an art gallery tucked away in a bustling corner of the city, where vivid colors and bold strokes adorned the walls, and the air buzzed with the hum of creative energy. Ashwin had wandered in on a whim, drawn by a flyer promising an escape from the mundane. As he admired a particularly striking piece—a riot of blues and greens that seemed to dance across the canvas—he found himself standing next to Aidan, who was passionately describing the artwork to a friend.

Aidan's enthusiasm was infectious, and his eyes sparkled with the kind of genuine interest that Ashwin rarely saw. They struck up a conversation that evening, effortlessly diving into topics ranging from art to life's little absurdities. There was an immediate connection, a sense of understanding that felt both exciting and comforting.

Eight years had passed since that fateful encounter, and their bond had only grown stronger. They had built a life together, sharing a cozy apartment filled with laughter, art supplies, and an impressive collection of books that threatened to overrun their shelves. They developed a deep love for each other, the kind that was woven into every aspect of their lives.

Ashwin's love for Aidan was a quiet, steadfast presence, like a gentle current that carried him through life's challenges. It was in the little things—the way he brewed Aidan's coffee just the way he liked it, or how he would stay up late to listen to Aidan's latest creative ideas, offering support and encouragement without hesitation. Their relationship was a tapestry of shared moments, where joy and struggles were met with the same unwavering commitment. But guilt would twist these memories, highlighting the missed signs and ignored warnings.

Aidan loved his alcohol and became a more gregarious and happy individual once the spirits were in. He would be more loving, kinder and just way more fun. However over the years they could both see that alcohol was turning from a source of joy and celebration, to a constant, everyday ritual. And because Aidan was experimental, he would even sometimes add other substances to the mix.

Every morning began with a sense of uncertainty. Ashwin would wake up and glance over at Aidan, trying to gauge what kind of day it would be. Would it be a good day, where Aidan was sober and focused on his art, or a difficult one, where the hangover from the night before left him irritable and withdrawn?

Often, our own behaviours reinforce our feelings of guilt. Guilt can drive us to act, especially when we feel responsible for others and guilty for not being able to help them. In such situations, our actions are aimed at reducing guilt by making amends, atoning, or even apologizing for things that don't require it. We place significant importance on the things we didn't do (or did do), which can overwhelm our thoughts and prevent us from taking the necessary steps. Our behaviour becomes a response to guilt and blame rather than the situation itself. The trap of guilt becomes entrenched when we focus on making amends or normalizing situations instead of evaluating our own responsibilities and the overall context.

The early hours were often the calm before the storm. Ashwin would make breakfast, the clatter of dishes and the smell of coffee filling their small apartment. Sometimes, Aidan would join him at the table, chatting about his latest ideas or plans for the day. On other days, he'd remain in bed, the weight of his addiction pulling him back under.

Holding his fork but not eating, he looked down at his plate and spoke to himself, "Somedays I felt like I was walking on eggshells, never quite sure what would trigger a shift in Aidan's mood. Small things—a missed call, a delayed response—could spark irritation, leading to arguments that left both of them feeling raw and exhausted. This was not the Aidan I knew. Ashwin's mind was a battlefield where these emotions clashed, leaving him exhausted and unsure of how to move forward. And then once every few months or so, when alcohol took hold, Aidan would turn into a little child – sobbing for his mother and wondering why she gave birth to him. His laughter turned into sadness, his creativity dulled by the fog of intoxication. I was discovering how much pain Aidan held inside him. On nights like these, I would sit quietly holding his hand or hugging him, watching as Aidan drank himself into oblivion, feeling powerless to intervene. How could I help him ma? What could I do?" tears rolling down his eyes and pain so visible for everyone around.

Another trap of guilt is taking on moral responsibilities in our interpersonal relationships. Our empathy can overpower our ability to recognise practical aspects, causing our behaviours to become stuck in a cycle where we fail to take productive action.

Yasha walked up and hugged him. Ashwin looked at Yasha and said, "The nights when Aidan went out without me were the hardest. I would lie awake, staring at the ceiling, waiting for him to return home safely. I would insist that Aidan take a cab or keep a driver for these evenings but he would not agree. He loved driving and tried to assure me that he had everything under control. I would message a friend or someone else who may be with Aidan to ensure they could accompany him. There had been many close calls and narrow escapes, but Aidan would always find another way to explain those away. And what a fool I was to believe him! And thank God I was with him that day at the party!"

Today, as Aidan moved from the hospital to the rehab centre, Ashwin found himself replaying conversations in his head, about quitting, going to rehab, seeking help from Alcoholics Anonymous (AA), Narcotics Anonymous (NA) or a therapist. He wondered what he could have said or done differently to convince Aidan. The guilt has become a constant companion, whispering that he wasn't doing enough, that he was failing Aidan and their relationship by not being able to pull him out of the depths of his addiction. The weight of his perceived failures ate away at him, whispering insidious thoughts that perhaps he was part of the problem, that his love was somehow inadequate. Despite his unwavering support, Ashwin felt as if he was watching Aidan drift further into a storm he couldn't pull him from, leaving him feeling powerless and alone in his struggle to keep them both afloat.

INSTANCES OF GUILT

Guilt is a powerful and multifaceted emotion that often arises when we perceive ourselves as having failed in some way, whether in our actions, thoughts, or responsibilities. It can manifest in various forms, each stemming from different sources and circumstances. Understanding these common causes of guilt is essential for gaining insight into our emotional responses and finding ways to address and manage them effectively. Below, we explore some typical situations that can trigger feelings of guilt, shedding light on how this emotion can shape our behaviour and impact our lives.

Perceived Wrongdoing

Guilt often arises when individuals believe they have done something wrong or violated their moral or ethical standards. This feeling can occur after lying, cheating, or unintentionally hurting someone else. For instance, telling a lie to a friend and later feeling guilty about the deception can create a significant emotional burden.

Unmet Expectations

Failing to meet personal or external expectations is another common cause of guilt. Individuals may feel guilty when they have not lived up to their own goals or societal standards. An example of this is feeling guilty for not achieving a certain career milestone by a specific age, which can lead to a sense of disappointment and self-reproach.

Harm to Others

When actions or inactions result in harm or discomfort to others, individuals may experience guilt, especially if they believe they could have prevented the situation. Accidentally hurting someone's feelings and feeling guilty for causing emotional pain is a common scenario that illustrates this type of guilt.

Survivor's Guilt

This type of guilt occurs when individuals survive a traumatic event while others do not, leading to feelings of guilt for being alive or unscathed. An example of survivor's guilt is surviving a car accident where others were injured or killed, which can leave the survivor questioning why they were spared.

Inability to Help

Guilt can arise from the perception of being unable to help or support someone in need, even if circumstances are beyond one's control. For example, feeling guilty for not being able to provide financial assistance to a friend in need can create a sense of inadequacy and distress.

Violation of Personal Values

When individuals act against their own values or beliefs, they may experience guilt for not adhering to their principles. This type of guilt is common when someone feels they should have spoken up against something that contradicts their personal values, leading to inner conflict and regret.

Comparison to Others

Comparing oneself to others can lead to guilt, particularly when individuals feel they are not measuring up or are more fortunate than others. For instance, feeling guilty for having more success than a sibling or peer can result in feelings of undeserved privilege and self-doubt.

Unresolved Past Events

Past actions that remain unresolved can cause lingering guilt, especially if individuals feel they have not made amends. Regretting past decisions that negatively affected others is a frequent source of this type of guilt, often leading to a persistent sense of remorse.

Social and Cultural Pressure

Societal norms and cultural expectations can create feelings of guilt when individuals perceive themselves as failing to conform. Feeling guilty for not fulfilling traditional family roles or duties exemplifies how external pressures can impact one's sense of self-worth and identity.

Parenting and Family Dynamics

Parents often experience guilt related to their children's well-being, believing they are not doing enough or have made mistakes in parenting. For example, feeling guilty for not spending enough time with children due to work commitments is a common source of parental guilt, reflecting the challenges of balancing responsibilities.

1. How do your own behaviours reinforce your feelings of guilt?

2. How often does guilt drive you to act, especially when you feel responsible for others?

3. Have you ever found yourself apologizing for things that don't require it?

4. Why do we place so much importance on things we didn't do (or did do) that overwhelm our thoughts?

5. How often do your actions become a response to guilt rather than the actual situation?

Acceptance

Embracing Life's Realities

> *Acceptance makes an incredible fertile soil for the seeds of change.*
>
> *– Steve Maraboli*

As dinner concluded, the family lingered at the table, reluctant to be the first to break away from the unity that the meal provided, despite the undercurrent of sorrow. Ashwin, feeling the weight of his family's concern and his own inner turmoil, excused himself to the balcony, saying he needed some fresh air to clear his head.

His mother, Sarita, approached him quietly, handing him a pamphlet about a support group for those dealing with a loved one's addiction. She suggested they attend the meeting together later that week. With Aidan in a no-contact phase at rehab, Ashwin found himself with plenty of time to fill, most of which he spent drowning in guilt. They would not have access to each other for 21 days, and Ashwin was eager to find a way to address his feelings and make sure Aidan returned home to a supportive environment.

As they walked into the first Al Anon meeting (a meeting for friends and families of addicts), Ashwin learned that drug addiction and alcoholism are two of the most destructive, life-changing diseases a person can struggle with. Also that it is normal for the partner to feel immense guilt in such situations. Hearing the group describe addiction as a disease was giving him a new perspective. He listened intently and noticed one word that was often repeated: 'acceptance'. The word intrigued him, prompting him to explore its meaning.

Acceptance required recognising that addiction is a disease requiring care and compassion.

It was difficult to accept this business of acceptance. He questioned whether acceptance was synonymous with tolerance. Would accepting Aidan's addiction mean allowing it to go on unchecked, to resign to a life dictated by its chaos? Did it mean accepting that there would be more instances where Aidan's life might be at risk? These questions left him feeling conflicted and uncertain, and he required a template to truly understand acceptance and learn how to practice it when Aidan's addiction threw curveballs at him.

Another member in the meeting interrupted his thoughts with their sharing. "Acceptance is essentially an emotional challenge. While it is possible to make a logical decision to accept an unpleasant reality, what is more challenging is to emotionally accept the reality of who we are, rather than the dreams of who we thought we would be. It opens the door to all the feelings of inadequacy, yet encourages us to continue living with the gratitude and awe that being alive deserves."

Through interacting with others in the group and doing his own reading, he realized that acceptance does not mean agreeing with or condoning events that have led to pain. It's about recognising the facts of the event in their entirety, including the pain they have caused. True acceptance is to let go of the illusion of control, learning instead to accept things as they are, regardless of one's feelings or moral judgments on the matter. By practicing acceptance, Ashwin could feel more present while making measured choices, while also not enabling Aidan's addiction. He would be able to see the situation as it is, allow complex feelings about it, and do what needs to be done, though it might be difficult.

Ashwin learned that, in a lot of ways, practicing acceptance was like dealing with the overflowing laundry basket in his room. Over time, clothes piled up, and though he knew the basket was there, he ignored the growing mess. Eventually, the day would come when he realized the corner of his room was in disarray, and he was running out of clothes. It was time to do the laundry. As he sorted through each item to wash and hang them, he acknowledged each piece of the mess, accepting the situation and the tasks necessary to clean up—much like taking personal inventory and accepting his imperfections. There were parts of himself and his psyche that needed healing, and by embracing acceptance, he began the journey toward addressing those challenges.

In relationships, acceptance involves understanding and embracing the other person's traits and quirks without trying to change them. It's about respecting differences and finding common ground. Ashwin learned that accepting Aidan didn't have to mean that he would agree with his every choice, but rather, recognising the reality of their situation and making the hard decisions together, operating from a place of love and care.

A profound realisation occurs when managing our guilt as denial begins to fade, and we start to accept how we too have been affected by the disease of alcoholism. Admitting our powerlessness in situations beyond our control can actually empower us to make real changes.

In terms of self-perception, acceptance is about acknowledging one's strengths and weaknesses. It's about loving oneself as they are and working on self-improvement without self-condemnation. Ashwin realized that accepting his own limitations and vulnerabilities allowed him to approach Aidan's struggles with greater empathy and patience.

Acceptance could be a powerful tool for Aidan as well, providing the foundation for his long road back to sobriety and freedom. Ashwin understood that taking the journey one day at a time could be the perfect way for Aidan to build a happier, more rewarding life.

Over the next few days and weeks, he accepted that they were dealing with a disease and began to understand the nature of addiction and the challenges Aidan faced. Ashwin resolved to maintain an open and honest dialogue with Aidan, encouraging him to share his struggles and progress without fear of judgment. He would offer support and encourage Aidan to seek professional help.

As Ashwin understood and applied acceptance to his life, he noticed that while the pain of the negative experiences remained, the inner struggle and suffering attached to them began to decrease. Acceptance became a tool for healing, offering a way to navigate the complexities of his emotions and relationships with a newfound sense of peace and understanding.

Ashwin gradually realized that he didn't have to be shackled by their collective past and its self-defeating guilt. Instead, he began to make conscious, albeit difficult, choices for himself and Aidan. Here's the thing: guilt can be deceitful. It exaggerates your mistakes, blows them out of proportion, and makes you believe you're a terrible person who can't do anything right. It's like listening to your worst enemy on repeat. And think about it—you wouldn't tolerate that in real life, so why accept it in your head?

Here's the secret bonus: letting go of guilt opens you up to a whole lot of positive things. It allows you to embrace the present moment, enjoy the simple pleasures of life, and build deeper connections with others. It's like shedding a heavy coat and stepping into the sunshine.

So, take a deep breath and bid farewell to that unwelcome guest named guilt. You deserve to live a life free from self-recrimination and regret. Remember,

you're not defined by what you didn't do or should've done, or even by your mistakes. You are defined by your ability to learn, grow, and move forward. Now, go out there and embrace the lightness of being!

As Ashwin drove to pick Aidan up after his 21-day stint in rehab, he was eager to see him again. This time around, he felt more capable of handling the challenges to come. When they met, Aidan looked healthier, but remorseful. Listening to him talk, Ashwin could sense that Aidan felt guilty too, about the pain he had put everyone through. Having spent some time reflecting on his own guilt, Ashwin felt deeply empathetic towards Aidan. He greeted him with love and affection, and shared his own feelings with him. For the first time in years, it seemed like the doors to communication had opened wide- they were both vulnerable with each other in a way that was reminiscent of their first few years together. As they talked, both of them felt a renewed understanding of each other and though the road ahead would be hard, both understood that accepting the situation was the best way through. They cried, embraced each other, but ultimately drove back with the odds on their side. They both knew they had a lot of work.

1. How do you currently handle situations that are beyond your control, and what changes might acceptance bring to your approach?

2. What aspects of your life are you struggling to accept, and how might embracing acceptance provide a path to peace and growth?

3. Reflect on a time when you resisted change. How might the outcome have been different if you had practiced acceptance?

4. How does your perception of acceptance differ from tolerance, and how can embracing this distinction influence your relationships and self-awareness?

5. What steps can you take to cultivate a mindset of acceptance in your daily life, and how might this practice enhance your overall well-being?

Perfection

Progress

11

Perfection

An Ideal or An Illusion?

> *The artist who aims at perfection in everything achieves it in nothing.*
>
> *– Eugene Delacroix*

Vikram was a man on a mission. At 32, he had crafted a life that could only be described as enviable. He was an executive at a thriving marketing firm, lived in a swanky apartment, and drove a car that turned heads wherever he went. His life was a perfect kaleidoscope of success, ambition, and carefully curated Instagram posts. If you asked Vikram, he'd tell you life was perfect.

Vikram wasn't always the epitome of modern sophistication. He started with a simple dream and an insatiable drive. Fresh out of university, he had big plans and a meticulous schedule that balanced work, gym sessions, and an expanding social life. He was the kind of person who inspired awe and a hint of envy in his colleagues. They admired his dedication and often sought his advice, though they secretly wondered how he managed it all without crumbling under the pressure.

As Vikram's career took off, so did his lifestyle. With a significant salary, he indulged in the finest things money could buy. His apartment was a luxurious minimal modern design, and it boasted floor-to-ceiling windows that offered stunning views of the city on one side and the ocean on the other. Each piece of furniture was a designer marvel, and his kitchen was equipped with gadgets that would make any chef green with envy. His wardrobe was a fashionista's dream, with the latest designer clothes that never saw a repeat in his social media posts. Vikram was always dapper, whether he was in a board meeting or at a brunch.

Beyond the polished exterior, Vikram was a bundle of infectious energy and charm. He had an uncanny ability to make people laugh, often turning mundane moments into delightful anecdotes. His friends loved him for his vivacious spirit and the genuine warmth he brought to every interaction. Vikram's joy was palpable, and it was this zest for life that made him a magnetic presence at any gathering.

Vikram's social media presence was constant. His feeds were a cascade of perfectly lit photos from exotic vacations, five-star dining experiences, and exclusive events. Invitations to elite parties and high-profile networking events became the norm. He found himself mingling with celebrities, top executives, and influencers. Vikram had become a true jet setter, hopping from one glamorous destination to another, always with a camera-ready smile.

However, beneath the polished surface, the cracks were beginning to show. Vikram's relentless pursuit of perfection was starting to take its toll. His days were a blur of stress and anxiety, each moment consumed by the pressure to maintain his flawless facade. The work that had once been his passion now felt like a never-ending treadmill, each step taken in the shadow of the next deadline. Finances to manage his lifestyle were a constant stress.

His social calendar, once a source of joy, became an exhausting obligation. Every event required meticulous planning, every interaction a performance. Vikram's relationships began to suffer. Friends and family noticed the change, feeling the growing distance as he became increasingly self-absorbed. He found himself in a situationship that looked like a relationship to the world but lacked the depth and connection he truly craved. At some point, the pictures he posted with the rich and famous became more important than the actual interactions. He would spend more time ensuring the lighting was perfect, the angle just right, and the moment Instagram-worthy rather than enjoying the company he was in.

Thomas Curran, a social psychologist, explains in his TED Talk, "Young people today are more preoccupied with the attainment of the perfect life and lifestyle. In terms of their image, status, and wealth. Data from Pew shows that young people born in the US in the late 1980s are 20 percent more likely to report being materially rich as among their most important life goals, relative to their parents and their grandparents. Young people also borrow more heavily than did older generations, and they spend a much greater proportion of their income on image goods and status possessions. These possessions, their lives and their lifestyles are now displayed in vivid detail

> **on the ubiquitous social media platforms of Instagram, Facebook, Snapchat. In this new visual culture, the appearance of perfection is far more important than the reality."**

As Vikram's obsession with every detail of his appearance and lifestyle intensified, he became fixated on his diet and exercise routine, pushing himself to unhealthy extremes. The facade of his perfect life began to crumble. His work suffered, as the constant need for perfection led to missed deadlines and subpar performance. His social media following started to notice the inconsistencies, and his engagement dropped.

Isolated and overwhelmed, Vikram experienced frequent panic attacks. The pressure to maintain his image led to dark thoughts, as he felt trapped in the life he had created. The once-vibrant man was now a shadow of his former self, consumed by the unattainable goal of perfection.

> **"You can think about it like a mountain of achievement that perfectionism leads us to imagine ourselves scaling. And we think to ourselves, 'Once I've reached**

that summit, then people will see I'm not flawed, and I'll be worth something.' But what perfectionism doesn't tell us is that soon after reaching that summit, we will be called down again to the fresh lowlands of insecurity and shame, just to try and scale that peak again. This is the cycle of self-defeat. In the pursuit of unattainable perfection, a perfectionist just cannot step off. And that's why it's so difficult to treat." – Thomas Curran

Vikram's social relationships started to deteriorate. His friends, who once looked up to him, now felt distanced and unable to connect. His need for everything to be perfect meant that he was rarely present, always thinking about the next post, the next event, or the next validation. Conversations that were once filled with laughter and genuine connection became stilted and formal, as if they were part of the performance he was constantly putting on. Even simple gatherings turned into photoshoots, with Vikram obsessing over every detail to ensure that his social media feed portrayed an idealized version of his life.

Perfectionism is, at its core, about trying to earn approval. The American academic Brené Brown, in her book Daring Greatly, writes that, "Most perfectionists grew up being praised for achievement and performance (grades, manners, rule following, people pleasing, appearance, sports). Somewhere along the way, they adopted this dangerous and debilitating belief system: 'I am what I accomplish and how well I accomplish it. Please. Perform. Perfect.' Healthy striving is self-focused: How can I improve? Perfectionism is other-focused: What will they think? Perfectionism is a hustle."

His professional relationships were similarly strained. Colleagues began to notice his micro management affecting team dynamics. Vikram would frequently redo others' work, unable to delegate effectively. This created a tense atmosphere, with coworkers feeling undervalued and frustrated. The collaborative spirit that once characterized his workplace was slowly eroding, replaced by a sense of competition and dissatisfaction.

In his romantic life, the toll of his perfectionism was even more pronounced. Vikram's partner felt neglected and undervalued, as their relationship became another item on his to-do list. The warmth and spontaneity that are vital to any healthy relationship were overshadowed by Vikram's constant need for control and perfection. Dates were planned with the precision of military operations, leaving no room for the unexpected joys of genuine connection. The intimacy and trust that once defined their bond were replaced by a hollow semblance of a relationship, driven by appearances rather than substance.

Perfectionism has been rising at an alarming rate over the past 25 years. Research indicates that perfectionism is associated with a range of psychological difficulties, including depression, anxiety, anorexia, bulimia, and even suicidal thoughts. Simultaneously, there has been an increase in mental illness among young people like never before.

1. How can the pursuit of perfectionism impact your mental and emotional well-being? What do you learn from Vikram's story?

2. Does social media play a prominent role in your life? In what ways do you think it has impacted your sense of self worth and identity?

3. Do you consider yourself a perfectionist? If yes, after having read Vikram's story, are you better able to understand where your own desire for perfection comes from?

4. Why do you think perfectionism takes such a heavy toll on personal relationships?

5. Are there any lessons you would take back from Vikram's story to understand your own journey better?

Progress

Appreciating the Journey

> ***Better a diamond with a flaw than a pebble without.***
>
> – ***Confucius***

Vikram's realisation that he needed help came like a soft whisper at first, growing louder until it was impossible to ignore. The once vibrant and joyful man found himself isolated, overwhelmed, and trapped in a cycle of self-defeat. One evening, after a particularly intense panic attack, Vikram found himself staring at his reflection in the mirror, seeing not the dapper, confident man he projected to the world, but a tired, anxious soul desperate for relief.

Recognising the gravity of Vikram's situation, his girlfriend, Priya, insisted that they take a vacation. She hoped that some time away from the pressures of their daily lives might help Vikram regain his perspective and find some much-needed peace. They decided to head to Japan for a week, a place known for its serene landscapes and tranquil culture.

When they checked into their hotel in Kyoto, a city famous for its temples and gardens, they noticed a small flyer about workshops in the neighborhood. Among the various offerings was one on the concept of Wabi-Sabi. Priya, intrigued by the description, insisted that they attend. Vikram, though reluctant, agreed to go along.

The workshop was held in a quaint, serene studio adorned with simple yet elegant decor. Natural light streamed in through large windows, casting a warm glow on the wooden floors. The trainer, a calm and composed woman named Keiko, welcomed everyone with a gentle smile.

Keiko began by introducing the concept of Wabi-Sabi. "Wabi-Sabi is a Japanese aesthetic philosophy that finds beauty in imperfection, impermanence, and the incomplete," she explained. "It celebrates the raw, weathered, and aged aspects of life, emphasizing simplicity, modesty, and the elegance found in the natural cycle of growth and decay."

She continued, "Wabi refers to simplicity, rusticity, and the acceptance of imperfection. It embodies the beauty found in asymmetry, roughness, and simplicity, often associated with an unadorned, unassuming lifestyle. Sabi represents the beauty that comes with the passage of time and the patina of age. It celebrates the weathering, the fading, and the transience of things, finding beauty in the worn, the aged, and the weathered."

Vikram listened intently as Keiko spoke, her words resonating with him in ways he hadn't expected. The idea of finding beauty in imperfections was foreign to him, but something about it was inviting.

During a break, Vikram approached Keiko with a mixture of curiosity and hesitation. "I've always been focused on achieving perfection," he admitted. "But lately, it's been overwhelming. How do you truly find beauty in imperfections?"

Keiko smiled warmly. "It's about shifting your perspective," she said. "We could choose to see an imperfection as something that needs immediate fixing, or we could choose to see it as just that – a simple imperfection. While one has the potential to put us into overdrive trying to solve a problem, the other allows us to reinterpret the same imperfection as something new. Instead of seeing imperfections as flaws, we could try to see them as unique characteristics that add depth and meaning. Every scratch, every mark, tells a story. In the same way, our personal imperfections and experiences shape who we are. They make us unique and beautiful in our own way."

As the workshop continued, Vikram found himself deeply moved by the exercises and discussions. They were encouraged to create art using natural, imperfect materials and to appreciate the unique qualities of each piece. Vikram's creation was far from perfect, but for the first time, he saw beauty in its rough edges and asymmetry.

That evening, Vikram and Priya sat together, reflecting on the day's experiences. "I think I finally understand what Wabi-Sabi means," Vikram said quietly. "I've been so obsessed with being perfect that I've missed out on the beauty of being real, of being myself."

Priya squeezed his hand, her eyes filled with love and support. "I'm proud of you, Vikram. It's not easy to let go of old habits, but you're taking the first steps."

On their flight back to India, Vikram spent time reflecting on what he had learned during the workshop. The serene landscapes of Japan, the calming influence of the workshop, and Keiko's wise words had planted seeds of change in his mind.

Back in India, Vikram reached out to the therapy clinic his organization has a tie up with. He never thought he would set up an appointment with them but he knew he required some help to embrace the principles of Wabi-Sabi into his daily life.

Stuti, his therapist, introduced him to a simple concept – progress over perfection!

"Progress is about learning to move forward, putting one step in front of the other even though you may not know where you may end up," she said. "It's about trusting your instincts and embracing the journey. It is about enjoying the fall if that is what happens."

Though fresh from his time at the workshop with Wabi-Sabi still on his mind, the concept of 'enjoying the fall' seemed not only utterly confusing, but absolutely terrifying to Vikram. "How can one ENJOY a fall, a failure? Isn't the whole point of doing something the fact that you're supposed to achieve something at the end? Isn't it all just pointless otherwise?"

Stuti smiled, realizing that like many other clients she had worked with, Vikram had simply never learned to revel in the process of doing something rather than focusing on the great reward of a desired outcome. She went on to say, "Think back to when you were a child, Vikram. Before you were told you were supposed to get good grades and plan for a future. Didn't you, like all young children, try your hand at painting, building blocks, and picture cards? What was the outcome of engaging in something 'pointless' like that?"

"Well", he said, "I remember those memories fondly, playing with my sister, doing nothing important for hours on end. The only outcome I can think of is that it taught me to love, care, and share. Oh, and also that games like that helped me develop the skills that are important for a child to learn at that age."

"So that was an activity that combined joy with learning, didn't it? And did you as toddler ever worry about the goals you needed to achieve? You just did it because it was fun, and even if you didn't do the best job, it did teach you what you needed to learn at the time, right?" asked Stuti.

Vikram shot back, "Sure, but I didn't have the pressures of the real world on me then. Or the ability to think as much. Now, I have work, social appearances, social media, and relationships to keep up with. And if I'm not doing a good job at all of them, what will people think of me?"

"What do you think people think of you now, when they find you to be a shell of your former self? When they see you break under the pressure of perfection? Do you think those who love you would prefer you to be happy and healthy rather than the perpetually perfect son, brother, friend, or partner?", Stuti said.

His eyes welling up, Vikram responded, "They are all worried about me. I see it in their eyes. I feel the distance between us. But I find myself incapable of letting them see me like this. I keep myself away because they may not love me anymore if I'm not perfect"

Offering him some tissues, Stuti said, "I understand how you feel. With all this fear and worry, I see that it's hard for you to focus on the progress you are making, regardless of the outcome. Do you see how it's holding you back?" Vikram nodded, looking down at his feet.

"Would you like to shed this burden, layer by layer, one step at a time?". He nodded again, still emotional, but now hopeful that there was a way through.

Over the next few months, Vikram would share the fears and worries of his daily life with Stuti. Like in most other areas of his life, he found it difficult to appreciate the progress he was making in therapy – progress that was intangible to him, but invariably present. Every time, Stuti would guide him back gently, reminding him of how far he had gotten from when he first came to therapy.

A few weeks after he started therapy, Vikram was assigned a high-stakes project with tight deadlines, and the pressure to deliver flawless results was immense. Despite his best efforts, he encountered several setbacks: a crucial presentation didn't go as planned, and a critical report had to be revised multiple times. The stress was overwhelming, and he felt a growing sense of frustration and self-doubt.

One evening, after another stressful day, Vikram sat at his desk, surrounded by drafts of the report and a cluttered workspace. His attempts to perfect every detail only seemed to make things worse. He felt defeated and disheartened, struggling to reconcile his previous insights from the Wabi-Sabi workshop with the reality of his current situation. The notion of finding beauty in imperfection felt distant and abstract in the face of his perceived failures.

Vikram called Priya, who noticed his distress. She encouraged him to take a break and reflect on what he had learned about Wabi-Sabi. Though he agreed, he felt the weight of his work hanging over him. He knew he needed to address his feelings more deeply.

In his next therapy session with Stuti, Vikram recounted his recent work challenges, his feelings of inadequacy, and his struggle to integrate the Wabi-Sabi concept into his professional life. “I thought I understood Wabi-Sabi,” he said, his voice tinged with frustration. “But now, it feels like it’s all falling apart. I just can’t see the beauty in all this. I’m too focused on how everything needs to be perfect, and I can’t let go.”

Stuti listened attentively and responded with empathy. “It sounds like you’re grappling with the gap between understanding a concept and applying it in real-life situations. It’s normal to encounter such challenges when trying to integrate new perspectives into your daily routine. Sometimes chasing the extraordinary blinds us to the ordinary.”

She guided Vikram through a reflective exercise. “Let’s talk about this project. What are the imperfections you're struggling with? How are they affecting your work and your sense of self?"

Vikram described the specific issues he faced with the project and how his relentless pursuit of perfection was causing him distress. Stuti helped him recognise that his fear of failure and the pressure to meet high standards were preventing him from appreciating the value of progress and effort.

"You're experiencing a natural part of the process," Stuti said gently. "It's important to remember that Wabi-Sabi is not about achieving perfection but about embracing the journey and recognising the inherent value in every step, even those that don't meet your ideal standards."

Stuti encouraged Vikram to focus on small, manageable goals and to celebrate the progress he had made rather than fixating on what was still imperfect. "Try to see each challenge as an opportunity to learn and grow," she suggested. "Allow yourself to appreciate the effort and creativity you've put into the project, even if the outcome isn't flawless."

By the end of the project, though it wasn't perfect, Vikram felt a sense of accomplishment and relief. He was on the path to integrating the Wabi-Sabi principles into his life, finding beauty in the journey and the imperfections along the way.

A prime example of Wabi-Sabi is Kintsugi, the Japanese art of repairing broken ceramics with golden lacquer to create beautiful, intricate patterns. Instead of discarding a damaged bowl, Kintsugi celebrates the imperfections and views them as integral to the item's story. This practice is believed to have originated in the 15th- century when the Japanese military commander Ashikaga Yoshimasa, disappointed with the standard repair of his favorite tea bowl, requested a more aesthetically pleasing method to restore it.

Wabi-Sabi, especially through the lens of Kintsugi, highlights the beauty in the journey and transformation of objects. A bowl repaired with gold, rather than being damaged, becomes more valuable and meaningful, though it can never return to its original state. This philosophy teaches us to embrace change and decay as natural progressions, encouraging mindfulness and a deep connection with the present. While wabi-sabi initially

seems like an aesthetic idea, accepting imperfection and the passage of time in our possessions can profoundly impact our mindset and self-view. In a world focused on rapid consumption and constant newness, wabi-sabi promotes finding meaningful connections with objects and recognising the beauty in our own evolving journeys.

With Stuti's guidance, Vikram slowly learned to set realistic goals, celebrate small wins, and thus keep his motivation maintained. This process required effort, to be sure, but he came to see that he was a lot calmer now than before. The pressure that he put on himself to be perfect slowly waned as he began to see all his strengths, wins, and losses from the lens of 'progress'. He learned more about himself and his own goals, rather than those that he believed were expected of him by society. This newfound openness made him feel freer than ever before.

The process of learning to focus on progress rather than perfection is not an easy one. Though we may all be

familiar with the idea that small goals and appreciating the journey are helpful tips to incorporate into our lives, it takes consistent effort to put that into practice. In this process, we may find ourselves returning to old patterns. However, the way through is to recognise what triggers our perfectionism and consciously remind ourselves at every instance how focusing on the 'now' is important. While one can do this themselves, therapeutic support can provide immense support in navigating the frequent triggers for perfectionism that come up in daily life.

Through self-work, therapy, and Priya's support, Vikram gradually reconnected with his family. At first begrudgingly, but then comfortably, he let them see his authentic self with little fear. His Instagram feed changed from expensive dinners and lavish trips, to pictures with his family and his newly adopted dog. He worked hard, but became able to take it one day at a time rather than burdening himself with lofty goals and expectations.

Six months after the Wabi-Sabi workshop in Japan, Vikram sat at the desk in his swanky office. Work had piled up while he was away on a family vacation, but he felt oddly calm. Reflecting on how this would have affected him six months ago, he felt grateful that he had taken the steps to change his life.

As he picked up his phone to check his messages, the wallpaper read – Chasing the extraordinary binds us to the ordinary.

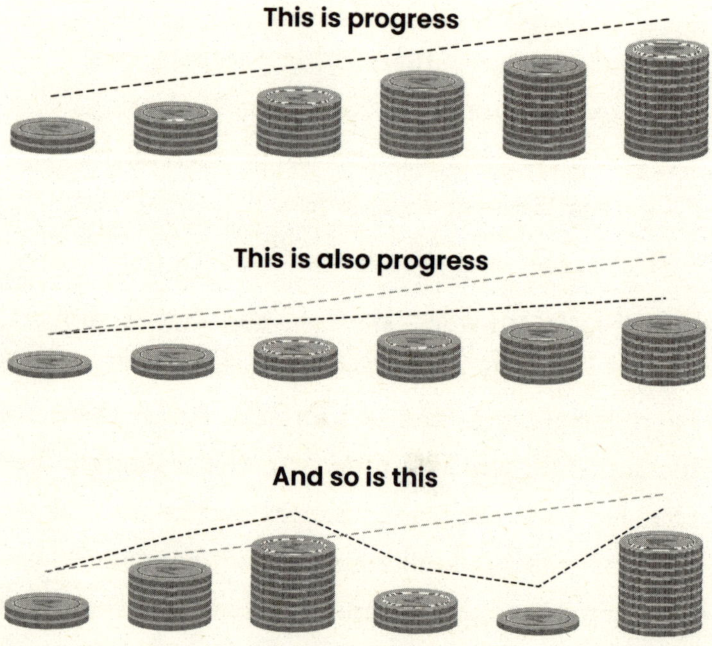

Define Your Progress

1. Why do you think the concept of Wabi-Sabi resonated so deeply with Vikram? What do you make of this concept?

2. Do you think embracing the cycle of growth and decay can enhance your own life? Why/Why not?

3. Reflect on a recent experience where you prioritized progress over perfection. What did you learn from that experience, and how did it contribute to your personal growth?

4. Why do you think celebrating small victories and milestones contributes to a healthier mindset and sustained motivation in pursuing your goals?

5. What steps can you take in your own life to build a supportive environment that encourages progress and embraces imperfection, both personally and professionally?

Frustration

Perspective

12

Frustration

Caught in the Middle

> *Frustration is the gap between expectation and reality.*
>
> *– Unknown*

Aman is a 45-year-old man living in a city that moves faster than a high-speed train. Raised in a middle-class family, he was taught the value of hard work, which seemed like a good idea until he realized it involved actual work. Aman excelled in school, went to an A grade university and quickly secured a stable job at a reputable corporation, much to the delight of his parents, who believed stability was the bedrock of a good life. He married his college sweetheart, Anjali, and they now have two teenage children, Arjun and Meera. Aman has always been the reliable anchor of his family, though these days he feels more like a rusting anchor on a sinking ship.

Aman's day begins at the ungodly hour of 6:00 am. His alarm, a shrill reminder of his unending responsibilities, jolts him awake. Before even considering getting out of bed, he checks his emails on his phone, already feeling the stress levels rising as if he's competing in an Olympic sport. He drags himself to the bathroom, where he stares at his reflection, wondering if he has always had that much gray hair.

Breakfast is a hurried affair – a cup of coffee and a piece of toast, both of which he inhales rather than eats. Anjali and the kids are still blissfully asleep as he leaves the house, and he envies their ability to exist without an immediate existential crisis. The house, quiet and dark, feels like a museum dedicated to the things he's missing out on.

At work, Aman is swamped with meetings that could have been emails and emails that could have been ignored. His job, once a symbol of pride and ambition, has morphed into a never-ending cycle of drudgery. He feels like a hamster on a wheel, only less enthusiastic. His younger colleagues, who seem to operate on a diet of energy drinks and optimism, are bafflingly efficient, while his bosses treat him like office furniture: useful but largely unremarkable.

Lunch is a sad affair – a sandwich that tastes like cardboard and a packet of chips that only serves to remind him of his cholesterol levels. He watches his colleagues take leisurely breaks, chatting and laughing as if life isn't a relentless series of disappointments. He often wants to tell his co-workers "FUC*&^ Bhujiya Khao!" but stops short and smiles at them without saying a word. It was just one phrase that was a code word between friends to say chuck it in the fu*& it bucket. Aman can't remember the last time he had a relaxed lunch that didn't involve multitasking.

Afternoons are a blur of tasks and emails that never seem to end. By 6:00 pm, Aman is exhausted, his energy levels more sluggish than the office wi-fi during a storm. He heads to a home that feels more like a halfway house, with family members passing by like ships in the night. Conversations with Anjali are brief and functional, often revolving around the kids' schedules or what needs to be fixed in the house. Arjun and Meera are engrossed in their own worlds, interacting with him only when absolutely necessary.

Dinner is a quiet affair, punctuated by the hum of the television. Aman shovels food into his mouth, barely tasting it, his mind elsewhere. After dinner, he retreats to his study, a sanctuary of sorts, though it feels more like a prison cell. He attempts to find solace in books or hobbies, but nothing seems to capture his interest. He often ends the day feeling more isolated than ever, his mind a whirlpool of frustration and regret.

We live our lives so carefully- trying to make the right choices and plan for our future. Yet, like Aman, many of us wake up one day to realize the life we were building all along has turned out to be unfulfilling. This frustration with ourselves and the world can lead us to a place where we find ourselves reevaluating the consequences of our choices.

A key reasoning error that comes up here is all-or-nothing thinking. Either we are raging successes or disappointing failures, life is either entirely happy or despicably unhappy. When this happens, it can help to view our lives in parts- where satisfying and less-than-satisfying parts can coexist.

Have you ever found yourself in a situation similar to Aman's? If yes, what were the feelings that came up for you? Did you find yourself engaging in all-or-nothing thinking?

Aman often reflects on the choices he's made with the kind of disdain usually reserved for reality TV shows. He wonders if he chose stability over passion, or if he simply chose the wrong path. His dreams of traveling the world, starting his own business, or even writing a book were all shelved in favor of a secure, predictable life.

He feels trapped by the expectations placed upon him by society, his family, and most harshly, himself. The weight of responsibility presses down on him, making it hard to breathe, let alone dream. Aman's marriage, once filled with love and laughter, now feels like a business partnership where the main topic of discussion is whose turn it is to buy milk. He feels disconnected from his children, who see him more as an ATM than a father.

Every evening, as he lies in bed staring at the ceiling, Aman is haunted by a sense of unfulfilled potential. He imagines himself in alternate universes where he is a famous travel blogger, a successful entrepreneur, or a best-selling author. In each scenario, he is happier, healthier, and much less prone to yelling at inanimate objects.

The frustration gnaws at him, a constant companion that refuses to leave. He dreams of breaking free from the cycle, watching instagram reels of interesting ways in which people resign from their jobs and finding a way to reignite the spark within him. But each day, he wakes up and follows the same routine, his frustration building like a pressure cooker ready to explode. He wonders how much longer he can continue like this, feeling more like a passenger in his own life than the driver.

1. How do you typically react when you feel frustrated? How does this reaction impact you and those around you?

2. How satisfied are you with your current work-life balance? What aspects of your job contribute most to your frustration?

3. What values or beliefs are being challenged or unmet that cause you to feel frustrated?

4. Are there any personal goals or dreams that you have set aside or compromised? How does this contribute to your frustration?

5. Consider your "alternate universe" selves. What would it take to pursue one of these alternative paths, even in a small way?

Perspective

Initiating Change

> ***Success is not built on success. It's built on failure. It's built on frustration. Sometimes it's built on catastrophe.***
>
> ***– Sumner Redstone***

Aman sat at his desk, mindlessly scrolling through emails when one particular message caught his eye. The subject line read, Wellness Workshops: Enhancing Employee Well-being. He rolled his eyes, already devising excuses to dodge this latest corporate initiative. However, considering his current state of perpetual frustration, he decided to sign up. Maybe, just maybe, it could help.

On the day of the workshop, Aman reluctantly walked into the conference room. To his surprise, about thirty colleagues were already seated, chatting quietly. He scanned the room and spotted 'Demanding' Deepak from the CEO's office. Deepak always seemed unruffled, a calm presence even under immense pressure. Aman often wondered how he managed to stay so cool. Then there was Sensor-Light Shweta, who only worked when someone crossed her desk, and Night Owl Nitya, her polar opposite but constant companion at work. Aman enjoyed giving people fun names, a quirky habit that helped him remember their real names.

As he looked at the host of the workshop, Pragya, he decided she was Preachy Pragya. Pragya stood at the front of the room, her serene presence immediately calming the room. Soft, ambient music played in the background, and the scent of lavender filled the air. A screen displayed the title, The Power of Proaction, in gentle, flowing script.

As everyone settled into their seats, Pragya encouraged them to take a deep breath and let go of the day's stresses. The room quieted, and a sense of anticipation filled the air. Aman noticed the diversity of his colleagues - from young interns to seasoned managers, all appearing equally curious and perhaps a bit skeptical about what was to come. "Today, we'll be exploring the concept of acceptance," Pragya began. "But first, I'd like to hear from you. What do you think of when you hear the word 'acceptance'? Can you share a situation where you're struggling with acceptance and why it's hard for you?"

Aman glanced around as a few hands tentatively went up. Pragya pointed to a woman near the front.

"Hi, I'm Meena," she started. "For me, acceptance means dealing with the fact that my promotion didn't go through. I worked so hard, and it's tough to accept that it wasn't enough." Aman nodded. He knew that feeling all too well.

Next, a man in the back spoke up. "I'm Rajesh. I'm struggling to accept that my parents are aging and need more help. I'm not ready to see them as vulnerable." Pragya listened attentively and then turned to another participant.

"Hi, I'm Arjun," said a young man near Aman. "I find it hard to accept that I can't control everything at work. It's frustrating to put in so much effort and still see things go wrong."

Anshul, a young colleague, raised his hand. "I want to share my story," he said. "For years, I struggled with my relationship with my parents because they couldn't accept my sexuality. I resisted accepting their viewpoint, and it hurt me deeply. I struggled for years with the pain of not being seen. But over time, I realized that I needed to accept the situation as it was. For my parents, it wasn't about rejecting me, but coming to terms with the loss of the individual they thought existed. This didn't mean I agreed with their stance, but I acknowledged their feelings. This changed perspective helped me find peace and allowed me to live my life authentically." The room fell silent, absorbing Anshul's honesty and courage.

Pragya's face lit up, "Exactly! What Anshul just spoke about – perspective – is something that goes hand-in-hand with acceptance. His story is a wonderful example of how we can tackle difficult circumstances if only we can shift our perspective and accept the situation as it is. That's what gives us the power to take action."

Sandra, another colleague, felt motivated to share her story. "I had a difficult relationship with my sister," she said. "We were always at odds, and it caused me a lot of pain. But when I accepted that we were different people with different perspectives, I stopped trying to change her. Our relationship improved because I was no longer resisting who she was."

Raj, a middle-aged manager, shared, "I've been fighting my declining health. I kept pushing myself, refusing to accept my limitations. But it only made things worse. Acceptance meant adjusting my lifestyle, which was hard, but it brought me relief." Another colleague, Leela, added, "I used to resist changes at work, feeling out of control. But once I accepted that change is constant, I adapted better and found new ways to contribute."

Anshul's, Sandra's, and Raj's stories highlight the importance of reflecting on circumstances that are in our control versus those that are not. Sometimes, we get stuck trying to change situations that are beyond our control, which leads to dissatisfaction. However, it helps to remember that even in such situations, a shift in perspective could change how we experience them.

Can you remember a time in your life when you consciously had to shift your perspective to adjust better to a situation? A nudge from someone to look at things differently? How did that impact how you experienced things?

Pragya then posed a question to the group. "Why do you think acceptance is so hard?" Several hands went up. One person mentioned fear of the unknown, another talked about the comfort of denial.

The discussion flowed with more colleagues sharing their struggles. It was a mosaic of personal battles and the quest for peace. Aman felt a growing connection with his peers, realizing they were all on similar journeys, facing different facets of acceptance.

Pragya gently asked: "Why Is shifting our perspective so hard for us at that moment? Why do we struggle and resist?

The room buzzed with a mix of vulnerability and curiosity. Aman felt an urge to contribute but hesitated. As the conversation unfolded, it became clear that taking a different lens towards reality is a complex challenge.

"It's like clinging to one idea of what life should be," one colleague said. "We set these high expectations and then feel let down when the reality fit into our version of what it should be."

Another voice chimed in, "Denial is comfortable. It's a safe space where we can pretend things are not as difficult as they are."

Pragya nodded, encouraging the dialogue. "Denial often serves as a temporary shield from pain, but it prevents us from moving forward. Shifting our perspective, on the other hand, requires us to accept that things may not be in our favor right now. It requires us to confront our fears and let go of attachments."

Aman thought about his own life. He realized how often he resisted acknowledging the truth of his circumstances. Fear of the unknown loomed large, and pride kept him from admitting his limitations. Ego whispered that accepting reality was akin to failure.

"It's also about control," said a colleague named Vikram. "We want to believe we can manage everything. Admitting we can't, feels like losing power."

After reading the perspective of Aman's colleagues on why we struggle to practice acceptance, what are your reflections?

Which of these factors do you personally relate to the most, and how have they influenced your ability to practice acceptance?

Pragya summarized, "Acceptance requires us to confront our fears and admit that we can't change the situation we're in. It's challenging because it demands humility and a release of control. But it's necessary for inner peace." She moved the attention to the slide on display which spoke about how to shift perspective and move towards acceptance –

1. Notice when you are trying to change or deny things that can't be changed. For some of us, the warning signs may be thoughts like, "This is unfair," "It shouldn't be this way!" or "Why me?" For others, it may be emotions like anger or frustration.

2. Repeat to yourself, "It is what it is," and acknowledge that you cannot change the situation right now. However, what you can change is how you perceive and respond to it. Remind yourself that you are not powerless.
3. Permit yourself to feel sad and disappointed; these emotions are healthy. At the same time, trust that acceptance will eventually bring peace and calm.
4. Engage in social support and self-care activities to help you cope with difficult feelings and improve your mood. Seek the support of friends or family, colleagues or a professional therapist or coach as the situation may demand.
5. Remember, accepting things as they are does not mean enjoying what's happening or giving up. It simply means acknowledging that you don't have control over external circumstances.

As Aman reflected on his own life, he realized his frustration often stemmed from his refusal to accept reality. He clung to an ideal of what life should be like, demanding too much of himself and others. This attachment prevented him from accepting his situation and acknowledging that though the situation may be hard, it did not have to be this way forever.. Ego and pride also played a role. Aman often judged himself harshly, unable to accept his mistakes and limitations. Acceptance would require him to let go of this judgment and see things as they were, without the distortion of his ego.

As the workshop came to a close, Aman understood that acceptance was not a sign of weakness but a source of strength. It was about recognising his power to shift his perspective and change his response to life's challenges. Maybe, just maybe, a new perspective could help him find peace amidst the chaos. He didn't have all the answers, but he felt ready to start seeing things differently.

Acceptance is a journey, not a destination. It's about finding balance in the midst of life's unpredictability. By recognising our limits and embracing our realities, we can discover a new sense of peace and strength

1. After reading this chapter, what does the concept of acceptance mean to you?

2. Can you recall a specific moment when you struggled with acceptance? What was the situation, and why was it hard for you to accept?

3. What are some thoughts or emotions you notice when you resist accepting a situation?

4. How much does the need for control affect your ability to accept reality?

5. In what ways do high expectations for yourself and others contribute to your struggle with acceptance?

6. Was there a person or event that helped you see things differently? How did this influence your approach to acceptance?

7. How can you remind yourself to recognise and accept things that are beyond your control?

Trauma

Healing

13

Trauma

Wounded Identity

> *Trauma is a fact of life. It does not, however, have to be a life sentence.*
>
> – *Peter A Levine*

This is a real-life story; one that would shake anyone to the core, but it must be narrated in order to understand a certain kind of extreme trauma and our responses to it.

In the heart of India, a young woman of 24, brimming with aspirations and the zest for life, embarked on what was supposed to be a routine journey from Lucknow to Delhi. Her goal was simple yet significant: to take an exam for the CISF, a step towards a future she had meticulously planned. The train, the Padmavati Express, was her bridge to a new chapter, filled with hopes and dreams.

But fate, with its unpredictable twists, had a different plan. On April 12, 2011, an ordinary journey morphed into a nightmare. She found herself face-to-face with robbers, a confrontation that could have ended with loss of her gold chain but her resistance and fight would alter the course of her life. In a cruel twist of events, her act of bravery—standing up to her assailants—led to a brutal act of retaliation. With violence borne out of desperation, they flung her from the speeding train.

The fall was just the beginning. Lying on the tracks, injured and disoriented, she faced a horror that seemed to compound by the minute. Another train, oblivious to her presence, passed over her, severing her leg below the knee and inflicting injuries that could have been avoided. The tracks, cold and unforgiving, became her prison as she lay there helplessly, pain engulfing her body, thoughts of her dreams and aspirations now distant whispers.

The darkness of the night enveloped her, but the ordeal was far from over. Rats, drawn to her wounds, began to gnaw at her injured leg, adding a layer of torment to her already unimaginable suffering. The vulnerability of lying alone, with no one to hear her cries for help, painted a stark picture of helplessness that few can truly comprehend.

Rescue came, but it brought little solace initially. She

was rushed to the nearest district hospital, a place ill-equipped to handle the severity of her injuries. Imagine the added layer of despair upon realizing that the place meant to offer healing and hope didn't have the necessary facilities to treat a serious accident like hers.

Shortly after, she was transferred to a larger hospital in Delhi, where she underwent operations to remove her injured leg and treat her spinal injuries. There, she faced the harsh truth that her life was forever changed. Imagine being in her shoes, wrestling with not just the pain and the surgeries, but also the feeling of utter helplessness.

Pause and reflect on all the thoughts and feelings you're having right now. What comes to mind when reading something like this? Some words that appear when we type 'trauma' into Google are shock, suffering, misery, wound, injury, anguish, impairment, damage, scarred, sorrow, and so on...

Trauma is more than an event. It is an experience that has a drastic long lasting effect. When we experience something; whether it's physical sensations or psychological disruptions, our brain quickly gets active to label and assign some meaning to the event and its impact. The adverse effects of such experiences are seen both on our body and our mind in the form of biological reactions, anxious thoughts, High amounts of distress or regulated emotions.

While all of us have different thresholds to trauma or what our brain assigns as trauma; It is safe to say that trauma occurs when our body and mind experience threat, overwhelm, disconnection, or a lack of safety or inclusion. Such experiences, although differently, overwhelm our nervous systems ability to cope.

This is an extreme incident and trauma with a big T destroying the very sanctity of her being. What would she have felt in that moment? Can you think of the small and big Ts?

Big T trauma includes major events that are rare but visibly harmful, attacking, and violent. These are life-altering incidents that leave a profound impact. On the other hand, small t trauma may not seem dramatic enough to be labeled as trauma by everyone, but these smaller events can eventually lead to a collapse in our coping abilities.

Examples of big T trauma include natural disasters, wars, life-threatening illnesses, accidents, and physical or sexual assaults. Small t trauma, on the other hand, can come in the form of consistent interpersonal conflict, emotional neglect by significant others or caregivers, infidelity, bullying, financial worries that threaten survival, chronic illnesses, and changes in life circumstances such as death in the family, divorce, or miscarriage.

We are often expected to navigate our way around small t trauma; however, if we don't address it, these experiences can leave a significant mark, impacting our reactions, coping mechanisms, and overall life experience.

While this was a big life-changing traumatic experience, trauma doesn't always come knocking with a big, earth-shattering event. Sometimes, it sneaks into our lives through experiences that might seem small to the outside world but are heavy with impact. Like when a child feels overlooked because a new sibling arrives, carrying the burden of feeling less loved. Or when that child becomes the go-between for parents caught in a never-ending cycle of arguments, mistakenly believing they must shoulder the responsibility for their parents' happiness. Or even the struggles that come with moving to a new place, where everything familiar seems worlds away, sparking fears that are hard to shake. And then there are the personal and family crises, like financial losses or living in a home where addiction casts a long shadow, shaping a childhood more than any happy memory could. These experiences, big or small, etch deep scars on our being, shaping how we see the world and ourselves within it.

It is crucial to know that trauma is in the way our minds and bodies process things, rather than the event itself. For one person, the arrival of a sibling, though difficult, may not mean much for their feelings in the future. For another, it may define the way they attach to people for their entire lives. The personal lens through which we view these experiences is what makes trauma so subjective- the timing, past experiences, our opinion of ourselves, the meaning we make of it – all play a role.

Whether it unfolds through a life-altering event, like that harrowing train accident, or a collection of smaller, yet significant challenges, like navigating the complexities of a dysfunctional family, trauma leaves a profound mark on us. It doesn't just touch the surface; it delves deep, affecting our nervous system, altering us physiologically, physically, and psychologically. Our bodies, in essence, keep a detailed account of every experience, as noted by the Dutch psychiatrist Bessel van der Kolk in his insightful work, The Body Keeps The Score, highlighting how trauma is etched within us. The personal lens through which we view these experiences is what makes trauma so subjective. Its impact is also heavily influenced by the timing of the incident. Traumatic experiences at a younger age can be particularly impactful, molding the development of the brain in ways that are lasting.

Our reactions to trauma—encompassed in the fight, flight, freeze, fawn, or flop responses—illustrate the variety and complexity of our natural defense mechanisms. These are not mere choices but instinctual responses to perceived threats, woven into the very fabric of our being. Recognising and understanding these responses is the first step towards grasping the full extent of our resilience. It's about acknowledging our inherent ability to endure, to adapt, and, with time and support, to find a way to grow from these challenges.

Trauma goes beyond just a single occurrence; it can deeply embed itself in our very identity, becoming a story we tell about ourselves right at the outset. We begin

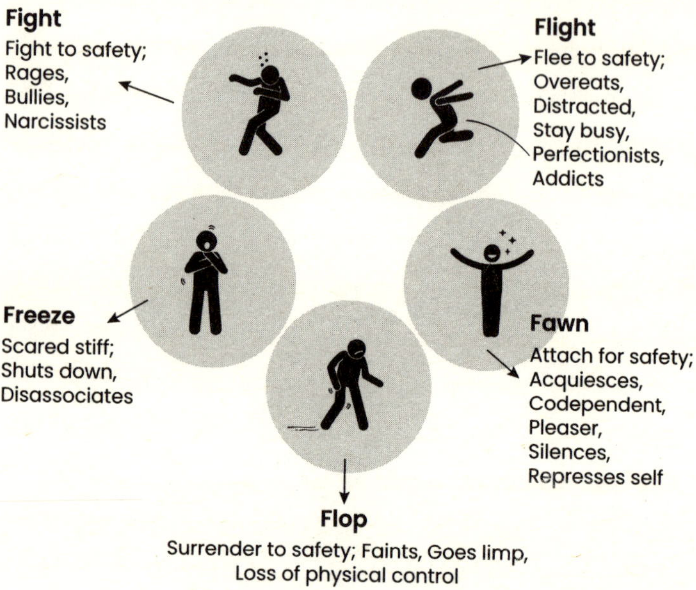

5 Trauma Responses

to see our traumatic experiences not just as something we've gone through, but as the core of who we are. This perspective can profoundly affect how we interact with the world, our relationships, and our self-view. It's a complex process where the trauma, instead of being a chapter in our life's story, becomes the title of the book. For instance, could the survivor from the story narrated earlier now simply be known as the girl who lost her leg? Is that to become her definitive identity?

Healing

Reclaiming Life

> “*Healing from trauma is not about returning to the old self, but rather about building a new self.*”
>
> ***– Unknown***

Is the traumatic event a life sentence or a lesson? For some of us it becomes our identity and we lug around the badge even when it's hard to carry. There comes a time when we have to work through our trauma and replace it from our identity with healing. Healing from trauma is a deeply personal and often complex journey, varying greatly from one individual to another. Yet, amidst this complexity, certain universal principles can guide the healing process, acting as antidotes to the pain and disruption trauma causes. It unfolds with the grace and complexity akin to the art of restoring a timeless painting or engaging in the practice of kintsugi. This ancient Japanese art form of repairing broken pottery with gold or silver lacquer is more than a method of mending; it is a philosophy that teaches us to find beauty in imperfection and to embrace the scars that life leaves us with. In kintsugi, the cracks of a broken item are highlighted, not hidden, filled with precious metals to mark the journey of breaking and healing. Each golden seam tells a story of survival, celebrating the item's history and resilience rather than its damage. It's a profound metaphor for the healing process, reminding us that our breaks and repairs contribute to our uniqueness and strength. The remarkable life story of a 24-year-old girl Arunima Sinha explains this concept beautifully. After a harrowing ordeal on a train journey led to the amputation of her leg, Arunima faced a monumental challenge. Yet, in the recovery ward of the All India Institute of Medical Sciences, a determination was kindled. Inspired by the Indian cricketer Yuvraj Singh's courage in facing cancer, she resolved to climb Mount Everest. Her ascent wasn't merely about reaching a physical location; it was about transcending her trauma, marking her path with the gold of her resilience, much like kintsugi. On May 21, 2013, as she stood atop Everest, Arunima didn't just claim a title for herself as the first female amputee to conquer the peak – she rewrote her narrative from one of victimhood to one of victory, a journey that redefined the impossible.

This narrative of strength and perseverance is a testament to the fact that trauma does not need to define us permanently. While it may be a chapter in our lives, it doesn't have to be the title of our book. We possess the freedom and the right to redefine ourselves, to change the narrative when we're ready. Just as in *kintsugi*, where the broken pieces of pottery are given a new lease on life, becoming more beautiful and valued for their history, we too can integrate our experiences into our being without letting them confine us. It involves embracing our scars, understanding that they are not just reminders of our pain but also of our capacity to overcome. It's about recognising that while trauma may be a part of our story, it is not the entirety of it. We can choose to fill the cracks with gold, to highlight our resilience and growth, and to move forward with our lives enriched, not diminished, by our experiences.

And all good things take time. One cannot rush this process. Time provides the necessary space and perspective for the fractured pieces of our being to slowly come together. It's a gentle reminder that the wounds we carry cannot be rushed or ignored. Instead, they must be tended to with patience and care. Healing is the art of honouring our own timeline, allowing the scars to tell their stories and the pain to dissipate gradually.

Engaging with our traumas, acknowledging them, and then deciding how we let them influence us is akin to deciding how we repair our broken pieces. Do we hide them away, or do we fill them with gold? Arunima Sinha chose to fill her cracks with gold, embarking on a journey that not only healed her but also inspired countless others to view their scars as markers of beauty and resilience.

The healing journey begins with understanding trauma, recognising its widespread impact, and identifying the signs and symptoms left by the experience or event. One of the most complex stages is overcoming suppression. Trauma often leads us to suppress, resist, and ignore what our nervous system is signaling. While this might seem like coping, it often results in dysregulation. Healing starts with relearning how to notice our internal cues and act accordingly. This process requires compassion, self-reliance, and a steady support system.

As we progress on our healing journey, the next phase involves stepping out of the survival mode and authentically connecting with ourselves. This is a challenging part of the process. We must rebuild trust in ourselves and move beyond the negative conditioning we've internalised. This involves understanding our desires, identifying where we feel safe or unsafe, and how we speak to ourselves in various situations. Trust, compassion, and self-feedback are crucial for authentically connecting with who we are.

The final stage of empowerment comes when we integrate a new version of ourselves, complete with new beliefs and ways of responding to the world and our inner selves. This is not a one-time activity but requires continuous practice. It involves consciously and deliberately building a safe feedback system within our bodies, developing new skills, and perceiving ourselves beyond the trauma we experienced.

Seeking support, whether from friends, family, or professionals, is not a sign of weakness but an acknowledgment of the human need for connection. These are the hands that hold us when we falter, the hearts that understand our pain, and the voices that remind us that we are not alone in our journey. There's an entire community of fellow travelers who understand the winding roads of trauma. Sharing your story, seeking help, and leaning on the strength of others can light your path through the darkest tunnels. In this light, our life stories are not written in stone but in clay, continuously shaped and reshaped by our experiences, choices, and the ways we decide to mend our breaks. Trauma may come into our lives unbidden, leaving its mark, but we hold the gold lacquer in our hands, ready to redefine our narrative, to change the title of our book whenever we feel ready.

Here is a three-step exercise for you to implement:

Step One: Take your time to identify the person you want to become. What qualities would you like to have? How would you like to view yourself? Reflect on who you want to be.

Step Two: Consider what actions, behaviors, or thoughts are needed to become that person. How would this person think, feel, and behave?

Step Three: Identify one action and one thought you want to start practicing today to move toward that version of yourself.

1. How do I currently perceive the impact of trauma on my identity, and what steps can I take to integrate these experiences into a positive narrative of growth?

2. What are some of the 'cracks' or scars in my life that I can fill with gold, acknowledging my resilience and strength rather than focusing solely on the pain?

3. In what ways can I practice self-compassion and self-reliance to support my healing journey, and how can I build a steady support system to assist me?

4. How can I move beyond survival mode to authentically connect with myself, identifying areas where I feel safe or unsafe, and nurturing my desires and self-talk?

5. What action or thought can I begin implementing today to align myself with the person I aspire to become, and how can I maintain this practice over time?

Grief

Love

14

Grief

The Silent Storm That Never Fully Subsides

> *Grief, when it comes, is nothing like we expect it to be.*
>
> *– Joan Didion*

He was here, and then, as if by some cruel trick of the universe, he wasn't. His routine was as predictable as an old clock—off to the hospital to see his patients, followed by lunch and a quick nap. He'd wake up to clear his emails and other assorted tasks, have tea and then sit down by the radio to listen to his favorite show 'Money Matters.' At 72, his eagerness to learn a new skill was laudable and the enthusiastic student would call the radio every day to ask his question. He took the COVID vaccine, a fever set in, it escalated quickly and the good doctor who was a bad patient was hit harder than expected. Before we could even grasp the situation, he was gone. Vanished. No fond farewells, no "see you later." It's almost as if he preferred it that way. When he was with you, his presence was unmistakable, filling the room with an energy so vibrant, you'd swear the walls absorbed his laughter. At parties, he was drawing everyone into his orbit with the skill of a seasoned storyteller. Yet, he was equally famous for his Houdini-like disappearances, vanishing into the night the moment he decided he'd had enough. His exit from life, it seems, was in keeping with his signature style—quiet, unannounced, and on his own terms.

The ripple effects of grief reached into every nook and cranny of our existence, subtly altering the landscape of our daily lives. My father and I (Saloni) would share the morning chai and go for our respective walks, then he would read the important headlines from the newspaper to me as I didn't have patience for negative news. We would share jokes and eat breakfast together discussing our plans for the day. The dining table was our space together. As we went about our respective days, he would observe but never interfere. If he saw me displaying unhealthy habits and behaviour, he would nudge me in his own way with a joke! Just a few months before his passing he would walk into my room at 6:30 pm and announce, it's time for a walk! It did not matter if

I was on an office call or clearing my mails. He was clear that we needed a walk to stay healthy and Work From Home needed a cut-off time. His presence was both a compass and a clock, guiding and timing our days with gentle precision.

Though grief is most closely identified with death, it can also come from various transitions that we encounter in life: a sense of being robbed or deprived of something that was once valuable – the end of a cherished relationship, the upheaval of a divorce, the void left by job loss, the vacuum of an empty nest or the disorienting change of moving to a new place. In 2019 when he had moved to Lucknow for work, I had felt the same grief. My therapist has pointed out gently that the emotion I was describing was that of grief and that is when I realized grief is more than death.

Grief is a complex emotion, a chaotic mix of sorrow, anger, despair, disappointment and, surprisingly, moments of laughter triggered by fond memories or just a sense of relief from the pain. It's a black hole that sucks you in, where time stands still and we experience helplessness like never before. For it highlights the complex path of mourning, where pain and love are intertwined, illustrating the deep connections we've lost and cherished. For some, grief is a sharp pain, felt deeply not just emotionally but physically, echoing through every part of our being. For others, it manifests as a thick fog, blurring our connection to the world and dulling our senses. It can reveal itself in unexpected ways: through an overwhelming urge to share our feelings with anyone who will listen, by adopting a facade of stoicism to shield those around us, or through sudden bursts of tears triggered by the most mundane events.

For me it was in everyday things – the meals on the dining table, the songs we had laughed at during our drives, filing my reimbursements in the office or making investment decisions. It was in the projects we had initiated together but not completed and it came up in every conversation around the topic of covid. I had unreasonable expectations of those around me, outbursts of anger, and withdrawal from things I enjoyed.

The Swiss-American psychiatrist Elisabeth Kübler-Ross offers a framework to understand the complex process of grieving. We each experience various stages in the grieving process, though not necessarily in any definitive order. Denial serves as a shock absorber, helping us cope with the initial impact of loss. It's a temporary defense mechanism where we may struggle to accept the reality of our situation. As the denial fades, the pain re-emerges, and we might direct our frustration outward. Anger can be aimed at inanimate objects, strangers, friends, family, or even ourselves. Post this we dwell on what could have been done differently to prevent the loss. We may find ourselves caught in a loop of "if only" or "what if" statements, seeking to bargain our way out of pain. As the magnitude of the loss sinks in, it's common to feel profound sadness, emptiness, and despair. This stage is marked by withdrawal from life and a sense of overwhelming grief and depressive symptoms. The final stage is about coming to terms with the reality of the loss. Acceptance doesn't mean we're okay with what happened, but rather that we recognise and accept our new reality and start moving forward. Sometimes we need closure to accept the grief but closure is a luxury for many of us. The person is gone, even if they are alive, and there are no answers to our questions.

We may not experience these stages linearly, they may be waves crashing at different points of time. It's essential to understand that the path of grief does not follow a straight line; instead, it ebbs and flows like the waves hitting the shore, varying each time in intensity and impact. As someone who loves the ocean, the metaphor of the sea offers a powerful lens to understand this big mix of emotions. These waves of grief often keep coming, each wave distinct with its own set of challenges and opportunities for solace. There will be moments when the waves crash against us with overwhelming force, high tides of sorrow and pain that seem to engulf us entirely. But there will also be times of low tide, when the waters recede, offering moments of calm and reflection. It reminds us that just as the sea eventually calms after a storm, so we too can find moments of peace amid our sorrow. Recognising these phases can offer solace, reminding us that all of that we're feeling is a natural part of the healing process.

Though many academic texts have highlighted the stages involved in grieving, one's journey through grief is deeply personal and unique. Understanding your own experience of grief can offer a chance to reflect on the rhythms it follows, and what works best for you to cope with it.

What do you think is your primary style of coping with loss? What are the things that have worked/would work for you?

Understanding that grief is a deeply personal experience is crucial. It doesn't look the same for everyone. For some, it's a tidal wave of emotions that knocks them off their feet, for others, it's a quiet sorrow

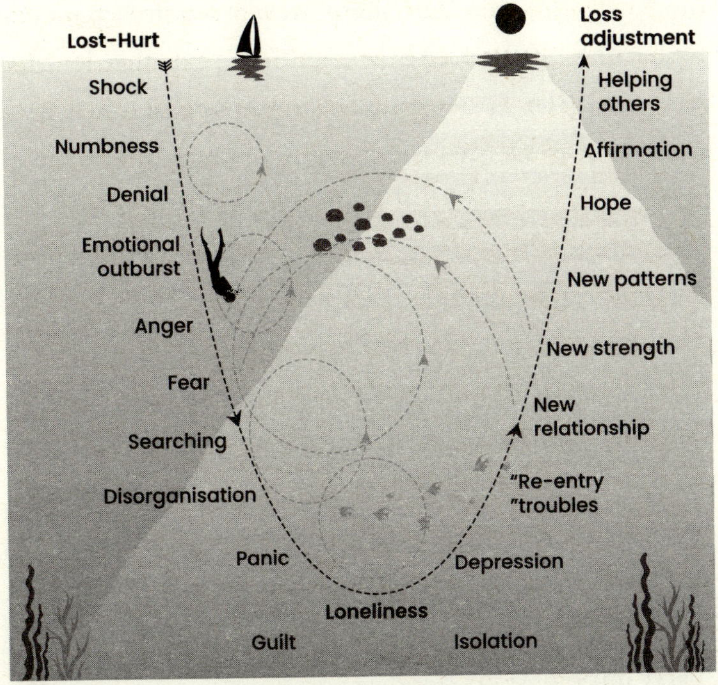

Stages of Grief

that lingers in the background of their daily lives. What offers comfort to one person may not resonate with another. This diversity in grieving processes highlights the importance of compassion—both for ourselves and others navigating their paths through loss. It's about finding what brings solace, whether it's sharing stories, creating tributes, or embracing solitude and reflection.

Navigating through these waves requires patience with oneself and the recognition that the journey through grief is deeply personal and unique. Just as no two seas are the same, each person's experience of grief is distinct, shaped by the depth of their loss and the nature of their love. Embracing the unpredictability of grief, understanding that it is a process that moves through us in its own rhythm, can help us find grace in our moments of pain as well as peace in our moments of calm. While most don't like the concept of a timeline in times of grief, I find it to be immensely useful to get over the debilitating phase associated with grief. I learnt the importance of the 13 days of mourning prescribed in our religious texts and how it helps us move forward and carry our emotions.

Culture forms an important part of how we perceive and process our grief. Because all of us exist in a context, psychology places emphasis on the integral role culture can play in helping us cope with loss. Hinduism, for example, views grief and mourning within the cycle of birth, death, and rebirth, offering structured rituals to help the bereaved navigate their loss. The mourning period, typically lasting 13 days, involves specific rites to honour the departed and support their soul's transition to the afterlife. Key practices include cremation, the immersion of ashes in a holy river, and the lighting of lamps to guide the departed soul. This period is a time for families to come together, reflect on the impermanence of life, and begin the healing process. Hindu philosophy, as seen in texts like the Bhagavad Gita, acknowledges the pain of grief while emphasising the soul's immortality and the importance of detachment. The rituals and teachings provide comfort, offering a path through mourning that integrates respect for the departed and insights into the transient nature of physical existence. After the mourning period, life resumes with annual ceremonies to honour the deceased, reinforcing the cycle of life and the enduring connections between the living and their ancestors. Through these practices, Hinduism frames grief as a profound journey of spiritual understanding and healing.

Even when we see loss coming—be it bidding farewell to a loved one after a prolonged illness or stepping into retirement after decades of commitment—grief can still take us by surprise. Understanding a situation logically and processing it emotionally are vastly different experiences. This disparity highlights the nature of grief: it mirrors the depth of our love while simultaneously stirring an emotional turmoil that disrupts our usual sense of stability. Such loss is emptying and life completely changes after this event, therefore, readjusting to new routines and ways of living are required.

Though many academic texts have highlighted the stages involved in grieving, one's journey through grief is deeply personal and unique. Understanding your own experience of grief can offer a chance to reflect on the rhythms it follows, and what works best for you to cope with it.

What do you think is your primary style of coping with loss? What are the things that have worked/would work for you?

The healing process begins with the acceptance that *some things cannot be fixed. They can only be carried.*

1. Have you experienced grief before? What does it look like? If you could use one color to describe your grief, which color would it be?

2. What were they like? If you had to describe them to someone new, which story would you recollect?

3. What emotions do you associate most strongly with your experience of grief?

4. Did reading this chapter bring up any feelings, thoughts or memories for you? How does it make you feel now?

5. Are there any specific rituals or practices that have helped you navigate through the grieving process?

Love

The Compassionate Companion

> *Grief is the last act of love we have to give to those we loved. Where there is deep grief, there was great love.*
>
> ***– Unknown***

An acquaintance sent this quote as a condolence message when my father passed away and it provided a sense of comfort at that point. I leaned on it, went back to it multiple times and understood over the years that love was the only way to move forward.

My father was my hero! He was my mentor, always providing me with the vision to move forward. I've begun to notice how his love has engulfed us even when he isn't around and is moving us to a better place each day.

The loving relationships he built over a lifetime surrounded us and a small example of the same is when his brother, my chacha, called me every weekend from the US for a year after we lost dad. The two of them would talk on weekends and that time was now mine.

His concern, his attention and the consistency of the check in were a result of their relationship, and now expression of love for each other. It taught me how to be present for someone and not be awkward in such a situation. We were both healing from this loss on these weekly calls. But can we really overcome the loss of someone or something that was truly valuable to us?

As they say in the spiritual texts, think about all the good things about the person or situation that has left us. This expression of love turns our memories into a fuel that propels us forward. For those who may believe in an afterlife, this also sends positive energy vibes to the people who are no longer around. People often say that I behave like my father, I move like him and make decisions just as he would. And everytime I hear that I send my love and gratitude to him.

Grief, with all its pain and heartache, reminds us of the preciousness of life and the moments we have with our loved ones. As we navigate this path we come to understand grief not as an adversary but as an integral part of our story. This narrative, though tinged with sorrow, is ultimately defined by love, growth, and renewal. It has the power to reshape our hearts and minds, teaching us invaluable lessons about the transient nature of life and the indomitable strength of the human spirit. It teaches us that we're stronger than we know and that love, in its many forms, is what binds us together, healing our wounds and guiding us towards the light.

We only grieve those we have loved- grief is only an expression of love that cannot be communicated to the one it is intended for.

Think about someone you have loved and lost- to death or to circumstances. If you were to write a letter to them, what would it say? What feelings would you communicate?

In the depths of mourning, love was the soft murmur in the silence, reminding me of the joy and influence my father had on so many around him. Given it was a time of isolation, building a memorial website for him was the most therapeutic process in this journey. Stories from people we did not know – his students, colleagues, random stranger were healing in ways I cannot express.

Psychologist J. William Worden's Four Tasks of Mourning suggests that we have tasks to accomplish in our journey through grief. Unlike a linear path, these tasks can be revisited and approached in various sequences.

These tasks are:

1. Accepting the reality of the loss, requires one to confront the truth that the loved one is gone and will not return. This acceptance is crucial for the healing process. Eg: visiting their gravesite or re-reading old messages.
2. Processing the pain of grief, involves allowing oneself to feel the full range of emotions that accompany loss, from sadness and anger to guilt and confusion. It's essential to work through these emotions rather than suppress them. Eg: talking to a therapist or being a part of a support group that helps you deal with the pain.
3. Adjusting to a world without the deceased, involves practical, emotional, and spiritual changes. This may mean

taking on new roles, forming new habits, or reshaping one's identity in the absence of the loved one. Eg: picking up new skills such as learning to cook or manage the finances of the household.

4. **Finding an enduring connection with the deceased while embarking on a new life, focuses on maintaining a healthy bond with the memories of the deceased while continuing to grow and engage with life. Eg: celebrating the birthday of the loved one in a meaningful way or creating a tribute that honors their memory. This task emphasises that moving forward does not mean forgetting; rather, it involves integrating the past into a hopeful future. By engaging with these tasks, individuals can find a way to heal and adapt in the wake of profound loss, creating a path toward renewed meaning and connection.**

At its core, grief stands as a testament to love. It reflects the depth of our connections and the emptiness left in their absence. By acknowledging and embracing our grief, we pay homage to our loved ones and the significant impact they've had on our lives. Grief, therefore, transcends mere loss, celebrating the richness and depth of those we've lost, and have added to our existence. It becomes a journey that fortifies our resilience, deepens our human connections, and affirms the everlasting power of love.

Love, in the face of grief, doesn't simply disappear; it simply shares the burden of our sorrow. It doesn't claim to magically erase the pain but rather, serves as a gentle force that softens the sharp edges of our loss. Love keeps the essence of our cherished memories alive, offering a glimmer of hope in the darkest of times.

Love is the bridge to the absent, sending heartfelt thoughts to those we've lost, and acknowledging the totality of their loss. With time's gentle passage, love becomes our anchor, empowering us to move forward while preserving the essence of those gone. It's manifested in the ways we honour them: sharing their tales, upholding their legacies, and keeping their spirits vibrant in our actions.

Consider a child who, in the wake of losing a parent, assumes greater responsibilities within the family. This young soul, motivated by love and the desire to honour their parent's legacy, might take on chores, offer emotional support to siblings, or even help manage household finances. Their actions serve as a bridge between the past and the future, ensuring the family's continuity and enduring spirit of the loved one lost.

Similarly, a partner who has lost their significant other might find themselves stepping into the dual roles of both parents, balancing the delicate art of nurturing with the strength to guide their family forward. This adaptation, fueled by love, is a poignant reflection of the partner's commitment to preserving the essence of what was while forging a new path for their family. It's a journey marked by challenges, but illuminated by the love that binds the family together.

The Dual Process Model of Grief offers a nuanced approach to understanding how we navigate loss. It emphasizes the importance of oscillating between two types of coping mechanisms: loss-oriented and restoration-oriented stressors. Loss-oriented stressors involve engaging directly with the grief, such as reflecting on memories of the deceased, expressing emotions, and participating in rituals of mourning. On the other hand, restoration-oriented stressors focus on adapting to life without the deceased by

taking on new roles and tasks previously managed by the loved one, such as cooking, managing finances, and rebuilding everyday routines. This model tells us that grief is an oscillation, a process of alternating between confronting and avoiding grief. At times, we may immerse ourselves in grief-related activities, while at other times, it's okay to move forward and take on new roles and allow periods of respite and self-care. This doesn't mean we are free from sorrow; rather, we are taking small steps forward after a challenging time. Guilt often becomes a constant companion, asking, "How can I even consider doing this when I've lost my loved one?" Yet, we must recognise that this is a necessary process. We understand that it feels burdensome, but we continue with the hope that it may feel lighter tomorrow. Healthy grieving involves balancing these two coping mechanisms; this oscillation helps us adapt more effectively to our new reality and navigate our journey of grief more adaptively.

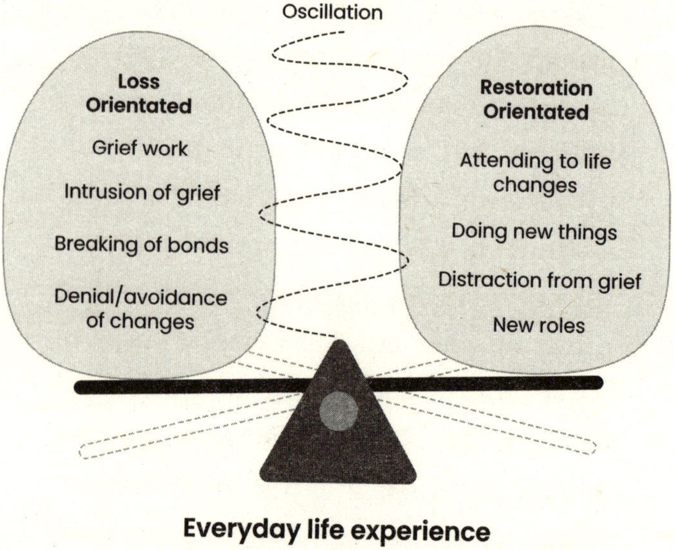

Dual Process Model of Grief

Beyond the confines of family, communities often come together in the wake of loss, each member stepping into roles that support and uplift those grieving. Friends may become surrogate family members, neighbours may offer daily assistance, and even acquaintances might step in to fill gaps left by the departed. These acts of love, collectively bring support that underscores the communal aspect of healing and resilience.

These examples highlight how love, in the face of grief, not only helps us bear the weight of our loss but also inspires us to grow and adapt in ways we never thought possible. It encourages us to step into new roles with courage, to fill the shoes left behind with compassion and strength, and to continue the legacies of those we've lost with honour and dedication.

Loss is one of the few universally human experiences that no human likes to think of. It is a terrifying inevitability, one that we'd dare not even consider the possibility of. However, when we see it around us, we often see people honour the memory of the departed in their own unique ways.

Reflect on these prompts:

1. **What I want to remember... Write about your last time with them.**
2. **What I'm going to miss the most about them is... Write about a time you recall them doing it.**
3. **What I don't want to remember... Think about the story you wished you could forget**

Through these acts of love and adaptation, we see that love does far more than comfort—it transforms us. It compels us to rise to the occasion, to embody the qualities of those we've lost, and to weave their memories into the fabric of our daily lives. In doing so, love ensures that those we've lost continue to influence and shape us, their presence felt in every step we take forward, every decision we make, and every act of kindness we extend. In this way, love becomes our guide, our strength, and our enduring connection to the past, as we navigate the future with resilience and hope.

Love cultivates kindness and compassion towards ourselves. It's the reassuring touch that encourages us to navigate this journey with grace and patience. Amid the waves of grief, love offers courage and hope. It's the faint yet persistent light guiding us forward, whispering, "You can endure," as we cling to the love that lights our way. Love, in its enduring presence, not only helps us carry the weight of grief but also leads us towards healing, reminding us that even in loss, the capacity for love and connection remains unbroken.

In the midst of grief, it can be hard to see any light. Yet, it's often through our deepest sorrows that we discover our own resilience. It's in the stories we share, the memories we cherish, and the love we continue to hold in our hearts. This love, undiminished by loss, becomes a guiding light, leading us gently forward. As time passes, our grief evolves, becoming part of our lives. It doesn't leave, we just grow around it, learning to live with it. We learn to carry our loss, not as a burden, but as a testament to our capacity to love and be loved. The memories of those we've lost become treasures, gems of love and laughter, tears and joy, an important part of who we are.

1. Think about someone you have loved and lost. If you were to write a letter to them, what would it say? What feelings and thoughts would you communicate?

2. How has the love you shared with the person you've lost influenced your relationships with others?

3. How has the love you received from the person you lost guided you through challenging times?

4. How have you grown as a person through the process of grieving and loving?

5. Think of practices in your own culture that are intended to help people cope with grief.

Gone From My Sight

– Henry Van Dyke

I am standing upon the seashore. A ship, at my side,
spreads her white sails to the moving breeze and starts
for the blue ocean. She is an object of beauty and strength.
I stand and watch her until, at length, she hangs like a speck
of white cloud just where the sea and sky come to mingle with
each other.

Then, someone at my side says, 'There, she is gone'
Gone where?

Gone from my sight. That is all. She is just as large in mast,
hull and spar as she was when she left my side.
And, she is just as able to bear her load of living freight
to her destined port.

Her diminished size is in me – not in her.
And, just at the moment when someone says,
'There, she is gone,'
there are other eyes watching her coming, and other voices
ready to take up the glad shout, 'Here she comes!'

And that is dying...

Epilogue

Signs of Declining Mental Health

Declining mental health often reveals itself through a mix of emotional, behavioral, and physical signs. Recognising these signs is the first step toward seeking help. If you or someone you know is experiencing these symptoms, reaching out to a mental health professional, trusted friend, or support group can make a significant difference.

1. **Lack of Enthusiasm:** One of the first signs of demotivation is a noticeable decrease in enthusiasm for activities or projects that previously brought joy and excitement. Tasks that once seemed interesting now feel like a chore.

2. **Procrastination:** Increased procrastination, even with tasks that are important or urgent, is a common early sign. This can manifest as putting off work, missing deadlines, or avoiding responsibilities altogether.

3. **Decreased Productivity:** A significant drop in productivity and efficiency can indicate

demotivation. Work takes longer to complete, and the quality may suffer as a result.

4. **Avoidance of Challenges:** Avoiding new challenges or opportunities that require effort or risk is another sign. Demotivated individuals may shy away from situations where they have to stretch their abilities or step out of their comfort zones.
5. **Feeling Overwhelmed:** A sense of being easily overwhelmed by tasks or responsibilities, even those that were previously manageable, can indicate demotivation. This often comes with a feeling of being unable to cope with demands.
6. **Negative Attitude:** Developing a negative attitude towards work, colleagues, or projects can be an early sign of demotivation. This might include increased cynicism, irritability, or a general sense of dissatisfaction.
7. **Frequent Distractions:** A noticeable increase in distractions and difficulty focusing on tasks is a common early sign. This might involve spending excessive time on non-work-related activities like social media, chatting, or other diversions.
8. **Low Energy Levels:** Persistent low energy and fatigue, even after adequate rest, can be a sign of demotivation. This can also manifest as physical symptoms like headaches or muscle tension.

9. **Decreased Initiative:** A drop in initiative and self-motivation is another early sign. Demotivated individuals may stop taking proactive steps or showing creativity in their work.
10. **Indifference to Success or Failure:** A lack of concern about the outcomes of one's efforts, whether positive or negative, indicates a loss of motivation. This apathy can lead to a lack of goal-setting and a disinterest in personal or professional growth.
11. **Isolation:** Withdrawing from social interactions, whether with colleagues, friends, or family, can be a sign of demotivation. This isolation can lead to further disengagement and a feeling of disconnection.

Recognising these early signs of demotivation is crucial for addressing the underlying issues before they escalate. Taking proactive steps to re-engage with one's work or activities, seeking support, and finding ways to reignite passion can help prevent a deeper sense of demotivation from taking hold.

Flip Words and Phrases

Hopefully you got the drift of Flip The Story – the narrative in our head needs to shift and there is one verb or action that helps us shift that narrative. Sometimes we have to push our minds to focus on the flip word and put it in action. According to the work of John Gottman and Robert Levenson, who closely studied the effects of negativity with couples, the suggested ratio is 5:1, meaning that for every negative encounter, there should be a minimum of five positive ones to counterbalance the effects of the first. These positive interactions could be in the form of physical affection, appreciation, validation, humor, acts of kindness, or supportive gestures.

The flip words outlined in this book are meant to be a gentle nudge, a guiding light to help you direct your thoughts in a fruitful direction as you navigate the ups and downs of life. However, they are not meant to be a replacement for professional help in case of a mental health condition. As professionals in the field of mental health, we urge you to seek help if you think you may be living with a mental health condition.

Now, enough from us and over to you. If you can, spend some time trying to locate your own flip words for some of the emotions listed below. Feel free to ignore our suggestions if you find better ones- after all, no one can know your experience better than you!

Emotion	**Suggested Flip**	**Your Flip**
Triggers	Glimmers	
Fear	Courage	
Doubt	Confidence	
Resentment	Forgiveness	
Sadness	Joy	
Frustration	Patience	
Apathy	Passion / Engagement	
Confusion	Understanding / Curiosity	
Jealousy	Appreciation	
Paranoia	Pronoia	
FOMO	JOMO	
Insecurity	Zoom Out	
Panic	Ride The Wave	
Failure	Growth	
Helplessness	Agency	
Control	Serendipity	
Chaos	Regulation	
Despair	Support	
Depression	Purpose	

Phrases We Use With Ourselves

Also here are some phrases most of us repeat and internalize. These are unhelpful phrases and if we flip them to positive affirmations, they help us move ahead more effortlessly. Self-affirmations have been shown to decrease health-deteriorating stress.[1] There is MRI evidence suggesting that certain neural pathways are increased when people practice self-affirmation tasks.[2]

Try to build your own affirmations below.

Negative Self-Talk	Positive Affirmation	Your Flip
I'm not good enough.	I am enough as I am and constantly growing.	
I'll never succeed.	Every step I take brings me closer to success.	
I'm a failure.	Mistakes are opportunities to learn and improve.	
No one likes me.	I am worthy of love and respect, and I attract positive relationships.	
I'm always wrong.	It's okay to make mistakes; they help me learn and grow.	
Things will never get better.	I have the power to create positive change in my life.	

1. Sherman *et al.*, 2009; Critcher & Dunning, 2015.
2. Cascio *et al.*, 2016.

I don't deserve happiness.	I deserve happiness and joy in my life.
I can't do anything right.	I am capable and can accomplish great things.
I'm a burden to others.	I am valued, and my presence is appreciated.
Something bad is going to happen.	I can handle whatever comes my way with strength and resilience.
I'm unattractive.	I am beautiful inside and out, and I embrace my uniqueness.
I'll always be alone.	I am capable of forming meaningful connections and relationships.
I can't handle this.	I am strong and capable of overcoming challenges.
Everyone is better than me.	I am unique and have my own strengths and talents.
It's all my fault.	I take responsibility for my actions and learn from them without self-blame.

Phrases We Use With Others

While our internal dialogue shapes how we see ourselves, the words we use with others shape our relationships and the world around us. Language is powerful—it can build bridges or burn them, depending on how it is wielded. Often, without realizing it, we use phrases with others that can wound, dismiss, or alienate. These phrases may stem from our own stress, frustration, or insecurities, but they leave lasting impressions on the people we interact with.

The good news? Just like internal dialogue, external dialogue can be flipped. By consciously replacing harsh, dismissive, or negative phrases with empathetic, constructive, and supportive ones, we can nurture our relationships and create spaces of trust and understanding.

The following section includes examples of common negative phrases we might use with others and suggestions for flipping them into more positive and productive alternatives. These are not about sugarcoating the truth but about finding ways to communicate that build connection rather than conflict.

Take a moment to reflect on the words you use with the people in your life. How might a simple flip change the tone of your conversations—and perhaps even the relationship itself? Let's explore how small shifts in language can lead to significant changes in how we connect with others.

Phrase	Suggested Flip	Your Flip
Be quiet!	Can you use a softer voice?	
I cannot deal with you!	I need a few minutes by myself.	
Do you need help?	I am here if you need me.	
Stop crying !	This is really hard for you .	
Stop complaining.	What's the solution?	
What a mess!	Looks like someone had a good time! Can we clean up now?	
You're so lazy.	How can we get started on this together?	
Why are you so difficult?	What's making this hard for you right now?	
You never listen to me.	Can we talk when you're ready to listen?	
That's not how you do it!	Can I show you another way that might help?	
Hurry up!	Take your time, but let's keep moving.	
You're always late.	I'd appreciate it if we could start on time.	
Don't bother me now.	Can we talk about this in a little while?	
You're overreacting.	Your feelings are valid. Let's talk about this.	

These verbs are powerful actions that can help transform difficult emotions into positive outcomes. We encourage you to reflect on these and discover your own verbs that resonate with your journey. We would love to hear about your experiences and the words that help you flip your story. We would love to hear from you and listed below are a few which we could not elaborate on in this book!

Write to us on appointments@reboot-wellness.com

Parting Words

> *"The whole is bigger than the sum of its parts"*
>
> *– Aristotle*

At Reboot, we create fun merchandise, and one year, we made a calendar with beautiful words from various cultures that promote the concept of good health. One of the words we found was 'nepantla', a term from Latino anthropology. Nepantla refers to those times between life's stages, such as moving from pain to healing, where transformation occurs. These in-between spaces, lacking clear boundaries, are where tremendous personal growth happens.

As they say in spiritual scriptures, pain is good. Without pain, we might do things that aren't good for us. Who we are Is a culmination of all the different parts of us. Each part of us is true, coming from some experience or learning or conditioning; but true, nonetheless.

And we as a whole are more than just these parts.

The essence of Reboot and of this book lies in acknowledging the multiple experiences, feelings, and patterns of thoughts that we human beings go through. The journey to change or heal or grow, begins from awareness, acknowledgement, and action.

Through stories and content, we hope to put forth the reality of being okay with not being okay. To put forth the humanness in being a human. The fragility of who we are strengthens through these very experiences. And all it takes sometimes is to just 'flip' the story. It is like having a switch button that needs to either go on or off for us to let go, bring closure or even learn a new skill to deal with life.

The thoughts in this book are personal, and we invite you to take what resonates and leave the rest. If the emotions you're dealing with become chronic and significantly impair your daily functioning or mental health, it may be beneficial to seek professional help from a therapist or counselor. They can provide personalized strategies and support to address underlying issues.

Remember the world breaks everyone, the very good, the very gentle and the very brave.

More available on www.reboot-wellness.com

Astha Ahluwalia

"The past 2 decades of my life have been dedicated to discovering, learning and advocating for Mental Health. This process has unravelled the depths of human experiences and revealed the value of ethical allied practices." Says Astha

Astha Ahluwalia is a passionate psychologist, therapist and educator whose work goal is to bring Mental Health to the forefront of human health and wellbeing.

In her practice over the years, Astha has worked towards building awareness about Mental Health in various communities and in 2017, co-founded Reboot Wellness to make mental health services available, accessible, and affordable for all.

Astha holds double Master's degrees in Psychology along with numerous other credits in therapeutic work and practice.

To take forward the work in mental health; Astha

- Engages with Corporates, Educational Institutions, Government organisations and various other communities to build advocacy for mental health;

along with helping people build resources for managing their own mental health needs.

- To bridge the gaps in field; Astha and her team have been working on building an army of equipped and trained mental health professionals.
- Astha's life purpose and soul work is the one-to-one deep therapy work with her clients and their families. Astha's work is all Heart!

When not working; you can find her travelling, always with numerous stories to share.

Saloni Malhotra

Saloni Malhotra finds joy in exploring new ideas and working on meaningful challenges. Whether it's through innovation, entrepreneurship, or collaboration, she's always looking for ways to make a positive difference.

Her most recent role was as Vice President at Paytm, where she worked on integrating digital public infrastructure into the platform to simplify daily life for millions of users. Before that, she led AGNIi, the National Technology Commercialization Program from the office of The Principal Scientific Advisor to the Prime Minister, during her time as Vice President at Invest India, working closely with innovators to bring impactful technologies to the forefront.

Saloni's entrepreneurial journey started with DesiCrew Solutions, a social enterprise she founded in 2007. What began as an idea to create white collar employment opportunities in rural India has grown into a company that employs over 1,500 people across South India.

Apart from her professional roles, Saloni loves supporting early-stage startups. She's an investor in Reboot Wellness, HelpNow, and Punt Partners. She also serves on the Board of Goonj, a non-governmental organization making incredible strides in grassroots development, and on the Board of Governors at IIT

Mandi's Business Incubator, Catalyst, where she mentors budding entrepreneurs.

When she's not working, Saloni enjoys spending time with her nephew Kabir and her two dogs, Idli and Layla. They're her daily reminders to laugh more, worry less, and enjoy the little things. She's also a fan of live music and loves discovering new artists or attending concerts.

Academically, Saloni studied engineering at Pune University and has enhanced her knowledge through programs at the Judge Business School, Cambridge University, IIM Bangalore, and a scholarship on Social Innovation from Sweden. She's also a proud alumna of the **Goldman Sachs 10,000 Women Entrepreneurs Program**.

She's been fortunate to connect with amazing people and ideas along the way, earning recognition as a **Fellow of the Ananta Aspen Centre's Kamalnayan Bajaj Fellowship** and as part of the Aspen Global Leadership Network. But for Saloni, it's never about titles–it's about the experiences, the learning, and the chance to contribute.

Saloni believes that even small innovations can create ripples of change, and she's always eager to listen, learn, and explore what's next.

You can connect with her on **Twitter (@ salonimalhotra)** or **LinkedIn (https://www.linkedin.com/in/salonimalhotra/)**–she'd love to hear your ideas!

Acknowledgments

A big thank you to our team at Reboot – Neha and Stuti for their contributions and helping with copious notes, edits and their patience as we wrote this manuscript. Their thoughtful comments, stories from the therapy room, frameworks to deal with specific emotions and most importantly the light banter was the fuel that helped us bring the book to completion. It was sheer joy engaging and learning from them in our one hour online meet-ups every other day for several months.

We'd be remiss not to mention our adventure to Goa during the last leg of writing this book. At this point, we had been working diligently on the book for several months and decided to book an impromptu Goa trip with our team to finish the book once and for all. That is where we found ourselves for the next week—holed up in an adorably cute apartment in the middle of the relentless Goa monsoon. As we buried our heads into our laptops, we had a steady supply of coffee, snacks, pizzas, and, sometimes, healthy, home-cooked food to keep us fueled. The only pauses taken were to play with the cats who'd visit the apartment, marvel at how much it could possibly rain in a day, and introduce some much-needed humor into the mix.

Those days in Goa were filled with laughter, creativity, and a shared sense of purpose. The stormy weather outside mirrored the occasional turbulence of our writing process, but it also provided the perfect backdrop for moments of inspiration. By the end of our stay, not only had we completed the book, but we had also forged stronger bonds as a team. This trip was a reminder that sometimes a change of scenery and a little spontaneity are exactly what you need to bring a project to life. As we left Goa, our hearts were full of gratitude and excitement for the journey ahead.

Big thank you to Aaliya, Vanshika, Shradhya for organizing the notes and chapters, the edits and their warmth. And for Pankaj who keeps us together and ensures we can do things we love with a free mind.

Also, a big shout-out to our editor and dear friend Hindol. His encouragement gave us the confidence to embark on this journey, while his patience and good humor carried us through every rookie mistake we made along the way. Hindol, thank you for believing in this project and for being the guiding light behind our words.

From Saloni: *Also a big big thank you to my friends from Cohort V of the Kamalnayan Bajaj Fellowship. I walked into* *the first seminar as a broken individual in 2014. At the end of the 4th seminar when we had to set up a new venture I decided to set up Reboot Wellness. While many discouraged me as I was not a psychologist and didn't have a background in this space, they encouraged me and loving showed up when we opened our doors. They gave me early projects, words of wisdom and their love. The poem on the next page is dedicated to Cohort V, our moderators Keith, Manoj and James. Most importantly a big thank you to the one who brought us together – Kiran Pasricha.*

Flip the Story

Tell me the stories etched in your skin,
Can you rewrite the past, find truth within?

What fuels you when applause grows dim,
When solitude calls, do you cherish within?

Can you sit with guilt, in quiet repose,
Accept it gently, without imposing woes?

Have you touched grief's core, embraced its shade,
Emerging anew, where love is made?

Will you rise each day, though weary and worn,
To find purpose anew in the breaking dawn?

Will you dance with anger's fiery grace,
And let curiosity take its place?

For in these flips, in moments small,
We discover who we are, our essence, our all.

As life's sculptor shapes with patient hands
Will you stand firm in the storm, as the masterpiece expands?

Trust the journey, let the story unfold,
Each flip brings you closer to the truth untold.